TO BOB —
A GREAT COWBOY FAN!

A Shrew Campi Lan
Bog Campi Lan

JERRY JONES
AND THE "NEW REGIME"
Memoirs, Recollections, Times and Travels with
'America's Team' and its most Notorious Cowboy.

TODD CAWTHORN

TTHORN PUBLISHING, INC.
IRVING TEXAS

TTHORN Publishing, Inc.
P.O. Box 630232
Irving, Texas 75063

©1995 Todd Cawthorn

All rights reserved. No part of this book may be reproduced or transmitted in any form or by any means, electronic or mechanical, including photocopying, recording or by any information storage and retrieval system, without the written permission of the publisher, except where permitted by law.

Cawthorn, Todd, 1966-
 Jerry Jones and the "New Regime": Memoirs, Recollections, Times and Travels, with 'America's Team' and its most Notorious Cowboy/ by Todd Cawthorn

Library of Congress Catalog Card Number: 95-90907

ISBN: 0-9649652-9-1

Cover and jacket design by Deana Galiatsatos
Page design by Merle Isaacs

Printed in the United States

—For my Dad, the second greatest pilot in the world

CONTENTS

Acknowledgments   *vii*
Introduction   *x*

1.	I Like My #!+&+@ Airplane!	1
2.	Lear 1 DC	7
3.	I Did It—My Way	11
4.	The Holdouts	15
5.	Born To Fly	19
6.	Jethro Had To Go!	23
7.	Is That Lake Mead?	27
8.	The Trouble Maker	31
9.	Number 22	35
10.	Time Flies	39
11.	Every City Looks The Same	41
12.	A Dumb Smart Ass	43
13.	Crossing The Line	45
14.	The Contrail	49
15.	"Ace" In The Hole	51
16.	Minnesota Mike	55
17.	Jerry's Kids	59
18.	Horns, Hides And Heads	63
19.	The Spirit Of St. Louis	65
20.	Wally...Er...Jerry World	69
21.	El Doradeer	73
22.	Mattress Thrashers	77
23.	The Lust On The Logo	83
24.	The Stadium Visual	87
25.	Jerry's Friend	91
26.	The Pride Of Port Arthur	95

27.	Mama Was Mad	99
28.	Hot Sauce Anyone?	101
29.	The 50 Million Dollar Man	105
30.	The Lottery	107
31.	The Devil In Mr. Jones	111
32.	Never Say...Never	115
33.	We Fly For Free	119
34.	Hoppin' Mad	123
35.	How 'Bout Them Cheerleaders!	125
36.	R-E-S-P-E-C-T	129
37.	Save The Children	133
38.	Damn Yankees	137
39.	The Silver And Blue Sleigh	139
40.	Staying Alive, Staying Alive	143
41.	A Little R&R	149
42.	The Voices	155
43.	The River	161
44.	He's Not Shy Anymore	165
45.	Lighten Up!	169
46.	London Calling	173
47.	Guns And Gauntlets	177
48.	The Quiet Assassin	183
49.	Never Again	187
50.	Everyone Beware!	191
51.	Performance And Paychecks	197
52.	Excuse Me, But...	201
53.	How 'Bout That Learjet!	205
54.	Cap'n Rick And Company	209
55.	Coach 'Em	213
56.	Happy Birthday To Me!	217
57.	Piss on 'Ya!	221
58.	First Time For Everything	225
59.	California Dreamin'	227
60.	Pasadena 1993	231
	Epilogue	237

ACKNOWLEDGMENTS

As with any creative work, there are many people to thank in the process of taking an idea and turning it into the book you are now holding in your hands. As a pilot, much less first-time author, let's just say that I was a bit naive. It was ten times the project I envisioned it to be. I never realized what was involved in writing and producing a book. But then again, I never realized what was involved in flying a Learjet for Jerry Jones and the Dallas Cowboys, either. Both of the above, at times, became hard lessons in futility and persistence.

I wish to extend my thanks to each and every colleague who played their own special part in this enormous project. Richard Anderson, Bruce Batman, Catherine Butschek, Elane Pearson, Mary Schust, Chad Milton, Deana Galiatsatos, Robert Love, Merle Isaacs, Sal Olimpio, Diane Smith and John Hervey. Their contributions are greated appreciated.

This book also would not have been possible without years of candor by Jerry Jones and his family, and to many present and former Cowboys players, coaches, staffers, and numerous others along the way, I thank them all for simply being themselves.

There is a small group of old and faithful friends who helped in a very important way, not directly with this book, but with life. To Chris, Nick, Chad, Ron, Chris, and Vance, thanks for everything.

And to several others—I wish to thank you for what you didn't do, and for telling me what I could never do. You know who you are.

A heartfelt and very special thank you to Ashlee for tolerating my insecurities, unconditional support, constant encouragement, and for listening. Thanks, Ash, for being my best friend.

Finally, thanks to you for reading this book.

INTRODUCTION

The Dallas Cowboys...America's favorite pastime. A Sunday afternoon football game in the United States boasts attendance that rivals major political elections in some foreign countries. The Dallas Cowboys and their flamboyant owner, Jerral W. Jones, remain in the forefront of professional football. From the 1970's to the present, the Cowboys have captured the hearts and loyalties of even the most casual sports fans. This book is not intended to be associated with Jerry's college roommate and the Cowboys former Head Coach—Jimmy Johnson. Nor is it one that deals with Jerry's fortune born of oil and gas exploration. All of those things have been well documented. However....

This is an inside view of "America's Team." They say that one never knows what goes on behind closed doors.... America's premier sports franchise, although successful, was not bought without a high price. Jerry Jones has taken the good with the bad, persevered, and come out a winner...to some. The bottom line is that as long as Troy

Aikman throws passes with pinpoint accuracy, Michael Irvin makes the impossible catch, and Emmitt Smith still runs his heart out, everything will be okay in Jerry's eyes.

One thing is for certain, no other owner in the history of professional sports has been more visible, notorious, controversial, or successful, in such a brief span of time. It is hard to believe that Jerry Jones has been at the helm and forefront for only six years. Whether one loves and respects him or hates and admonishes him, the Cowboys record under his "socks to jocks" leadership speaks for itself. As an integral and often overlooked part of the Cowboys organization, I was along for the not so smooth ride as the "New Regime" climbed from the cellar to the Super Bowl. I flew the Dallas Cowboys private Learjet. I flew the Troy Aikmans and the Emmitt Smiths. I flew everyone, everywhere, and I flew often.

Twenty plus days a month I watched, listened, and was involved as Jerry and Jimmy rebuilt the once proud Dallas Cowboys. It was a long hard road for everyone and they had to get there by air. There is so much more to the "Silver and Blue" than anyone would ever believe. The innermost sanctum of the new Cowboys "family" has never been revealed until now. Sometimes I had a hard time believing it, too. My private view of Jerry Jones and the National Football League from 35,000 feet proves that truth really is stranger than fiction.

I always wanted to be a pilot. I never knew anything different than airplanes, flying, and the aviator's lifestyle. In fact, on the day I was born my father was on a flight as a pilot for the now defunct Eastern Airlines. He was hired on September 9, 1963, and I was born on October 24, 1966. I was the eldest of three boys. My father had been on reserve while he and my mom waited anxiously for my arrival during that week, but nothing happened. The next week crew scheduling called and said that he was needed to fly a two-day trip. He asked her to call him if anything happened and he would come home immediately.

The flight departed Atlanta and flew to New York. As the passengers deplaned, my dad ran into Eastern's flight operations and called home. Nothing. They left that afternoon and continued the flight to Montreal, Canada. As soon as they arrived and were checked into the hotel, he called home again. Mom had gone to the hospital and a little aviator was on the way.

It was then 9:30 p.m. Unfortunately, his flight into Montreal that night was the last one in or out for the evening. He was unable to return to Georgia. The following morning he checked all of the departing flights to Atlanta and thought the easiest way for him to get back was to continue flying the trip. Before departure, he called the hospital. Nothing. They departed Montreal and flew back to New York. Still nothing.

The flight continued non-stop from New York to Miami International. He rechecked the flights, but with the layovers and waiting periods his best bet was simply to continue the flight. Upon arrival in Miami, he called again. Nothing. One more leg and he would be home in Atlanta. They departed Miami around 3:30 p.m. and headed home. The flight arrived around 5:00 p.m. and he hastily drove to the hospital. He arrived at the hospital around 6:15 p.m. and I arrived shortly thereafter at 6:34 p.m.!

Several years later my parents purchased a small lakefront cabin in the sleepy little town of Hartwell in Northeast Georgia. We still lived in Atlanta but we frequented the lake often, especially during the summer. It was during one of our summer weekends on the lake that a longtime friend of my father's, Al Weaver, a fellow Eastern pilot, flew up to visit. He landed on a small grass airstrip in his four seat Piper Cherokee 140. My dad and I, as well as Al and his son, climbed in and went for a joy ride around the lake. I was fascinated.

I remember leaning forward, and with bated breath I exclaimed that "This was it!" This was what I wanted to be when I grew up. They looked at each other and smiled, they knew exactly how I felt. They never forgot what I said. I never forgot it, either. Shortly afterward, my father arranged a field trip for all of my young classmates to Atlanta Hartsfield International Airport. We went through all of the airplanes, met the pilots, watched and listened. I didn't care about the cabin of the airplane because I knew my seat was in the cockpit. There sure were a lot of clocks up there I thought.

Twelve years later, my Commercial Pilot and Flight Instructor licenses were complete. I was also in the process of completing the requirements for my Aviation Administration Degree at Miami/Dade College in Miami, Florida. I attended the School of Aviation and Aerospace Studies while I worked as a free-lance Flight Instructor and part-time with a local air charter company. I even flew parachutists on the weekends.

I was looking forward to favorable responses from the many corporate flight departments and commuter airlines that I had sent resumes. I began talking to Ark-Air Flight, Inc., the Cowboys flight department and their Chief Pilot, Eddy Collins, in March of 1990.

Due to the schedule that Jerry Jones flew, he had managed to go through four pilots in less than two years.

I didn't care. I was young, ambitious, and willing to sacrifice. I fit the mold and it was the chance of a lifetime....

Years earlier, Jerry Jones operated turboprop King Airs. He had always owned airplanes because they were necessary for his numerous oil and gas operations. Jerry finally outgrew the capabilities of the turboprop and a Learjet was purchased. Eddy had basically flown the King Air as a single pilot operation. I still don't know how he did it.

The new Learjet required a two-man flight crew. Jerry sent Eddy and Al for training at Simuflite Training International, located at the Dallas/Fort Worth International Airport. Al Devens was retired from the United States Air Force. He had flown everything from B-25s to B-52s. He was highly experienced, very disciplined, and he did whatever it took to get the job done. Although Jerry had two veteran pilots at the controls of his Lear, he still felt uncomfortable. His entire family would be onboard and he needed some peace of mind.

A Learjet "guru" by the name of Lee Sewell was hired to fly with Eddy and Al during the first six months of operation. Lee had been hired by Southwest Airlines in the fall of that same year but his class date for training and orientation did not begin until the following February. It was the ideal situation for everyone. Eddy and Al were able to learn from a high-time Lear pilot that knew the airplane inside and out and Jerry felt comfortable knowing that someone in the front was fully capable in the difficult and unforgiving "Fearjet."

Eddy and Al had gone through a program of intense ground, systems, and simulator training at Simuflite but it still took time in an unfamiliar airplane for them to "get up to speed." Lee gained employment for six months in the interim and they ironed out a lot of the problems in the airplane. Finally, everyone involved had begun to feel comfortable, except Lee. It only took six months for him to see the writing on the wall. He had done a tremendous job of coaching. He was tired but everyone was pleased. Lee's dream of becoming an airline pilot was drawing near and Eddy soon realized that a three man flight department was necessary.

Even prior to the Cowboys, Jerry and the Joneses flew an unbelievable schedule. Jerry asked, "Lee, what would it take for you to forego your career at Southwest and come onboard full-time with us?" Lee had definitely seen the light, he had been in corporate aviation far too long. Jerry's habits only reinforced his decision. "You don't have enough money," he replied. Lee had aspirations of his own and is now a captain with Southwest. I flew with Lee several times, he is a good pilot and a good friend.

In anticipation of Lee's departure, Eddy had been in contact with several pilots in Little Rock. The next fella to become part of Ark-Air Flight, Inc. was Kirk Spangler. An experienced jet pilot, Kirk flew for a small company based in Little Rock. Eddy had talked so positively with him about the opening that he persuaded Kirk to quit his job and come onboard. Afterwards, Jerry decided he didn't want to hire him which left Kirk in a bad situation. He received the "runaround" from Eddy so he went to Jerry and explained his plight. Jerry agreed.

Kirk was hired, trained at Simuflite, and received his type rating in the Learjet. Less than one year later, the schedule that he had flown basically ended his marriage. He had a young son and his only hopes of salvaging any semblance of a home life meant that decisions had to be made. Kirk decided that he would be better off free-lance flying in the Little Rock area. It was not the most popular decision, Jerry should know about that. It costs several thousand dollars to send a pilot to school at Simuflite, Jerry had invested a lot of money in Kirk. Almost one year later he abruptly quit. He is now flying for Southwest Airlines.

Next on the list was Jeff Cook. He was another hard working young pilot that was climbing his way through the ranks. He had even fueled airplanes in Little Rock with the hope of gaining employment with a flight crew in need. His prayers were finally answered. Eddy offered him a job and he was hired in November of 1988. Three months later an agreement was reached with "Bum" Bright. Jerry Jones now owned the Dallas Cowboys. A "New Regime" a brash new owner, and an almost entirely new staff moved into the club's posh facilities in Valley Ranch. Their first year was a well-documented fiasco.

The hapless and overworked flight crew flew well over 900 hours during the course of 1989. That is truly an astronomical amount of time in a Learjet. They were never home and they flew all day and all night it seemed. It was a bruising schedule with no F.A.A. regulations. Time was of the essence and common sense had taken a back seat. There are no guidelines for privately flown aircraft...there should be. They flew until tensions were high, conditions were unbearable, and Jeff could not take it any longer. He began his interviews with several major airlines while his relationship with Eddy, Al, and Jerry rapidly deteriorated. Jeff felt the schedule they flew was unsafe.

Jeff had one last chance. Jerry and Eddy put the squeeze on him. "If you will sign a contract, we will keep you on and we will pay for your type rating," they said. In other words, they would upgrade him from co-pilot to captain on the Lear. "Otherwise, we're going to let you go," came the ultimatum. He was floored, he had put his heart, soul, and life on the line. He too had hopes of realizing his dream of becoming an airline pilot.

After a year of nonstop flying they wanted Jeff to sign a work contract! He knew that he had airline interviews, he thought about it and came to a decision. "Consider me unemployed," he said. He removed his electronic ball and chain, otherwise known as a beeper, and laid it on the table. Enough was enough. He was unable and unwilling to keep up with Jerry Jones any longer. The Cowboys had begun the now-familiar process of hiring someone else.

The Learjet was based at Dallas Love Field Airport. Jet East was the airplane's new home. In early 1990, at the time I was inquiring about the job, word quickly spread that the Cowboys were looking for a new pilot. One of the pilots at Jet East told Eddy and Al that a good friend of his was an ex-Braniff captain that also had flight time in Learjets. Jerry agreed to hire him and he flew an orientation flight with Eddy prior to his training at Simuflite. He was hired shortly before me so I thought my chances of employment with the Cowboys were gone. I was wrong.

Eddy and pilot #4 departed on Thursday and flew a three day trip. It was an opportunity for him to re-familiarize himself with the Lear and check out Jerry Jones operation. They returned to Dallas late on Sunday night and he was scheduled to begin his training at Simuflite the next day. On Monday morning, Eddy and Al were waiting at Jet East for their departure to San Francisco. At 11:00 a.m. pilot #4 walked in. "Hey, aren't you supposed to be in school?" they asked." "I quit," he said. No explanation was necessary, they knew why.

Four pilots with tours of duty ranging from three days to six months to one year. No one was able to keep up with Jerry and the Joneses. The schedule was simply too much. It only took him three days to realize that the Cowboys and Jerry Jones were not for him. He wanted no part of it. Eddy and Al flew to San Francisco. On the way they talked about the young fella back in Georgia. He was willing to sign a three-year contract, he was eager, and he would work for peanuts. Jerry wanted a signed work contract because he was tired of paying big dollars then being left with nothing.

They had my resume and on the night of April 2, 1990, I received a phone call. It was the strangest thing, because one year prior it seemed as though I had actually seen into the future. One afternoon I was at the Tamiami Airport in Miami, Florida, meeting someone at the Tamiami Jet Center. It was during the spring of 1989 while I was still in college. As I walked into the terminal I was surprised to see a cream-colored Lear 35 sitting outside on the tarmac.

The Tamiami Airport did not experience a lot of jet traffic, due to the flight school's presence. It was mainly a flight training and small corporate airport. The Lear's call letters were N555GB. Upon closer examination, I noticed that a small and inconspicuous Dallas Cowboys helmet sticker was positioned on the tail. It was barely visible. Being a fan all of my life it dawned on me, that Lear was either the Dallas Cowboys or possibly a charter. It was in Miami picking up new head coach Jimmy Johnson and his coaching staff. I didn't know at the time, but Eddy and Al were waiting at the airport that day.

Now, in the spring of 1990, I was back at home in Georgia when Eddy called. "Todd, did you see the movie Wall Street?" he asked. "Yes," I replied. "Do you remember the scene where Michael Douglas told the young and upcoming Charlie Sheen that there was a world to conquer and this was his wake up call?" he asked. "Yes sir," I replied in disbelief. "Well, this is your wake up call," he said. We talked for almost 30 minutes. When I hung up the phone I sat there for a second, then I screamed loud enough that I almost scared my parents to death.

I was a pilot for the Dallas Cowboys! It was the most thrilling day of my young life and I will never forget it. My dreams had come true and all of my hard work had finally paid off. The events that followed happened very rapidly. They needed me in Dallas within two weeks to begin my jet training at Simuflite. Fortunately, my Aunt Louise and several of my relatives lived in Dallas. I could stay with her temporarily. I knew no one in "Big D" I had only flown through a few times. Little did I know, that was all I would be doing for the next three years anyway.

I had been in Dallas for three days when Eddy arranged for me to meet my infamous new boss. It was also a chance for me to meet captain Al Devens. They were flying into Dallas from Little Rock with Jerry, his wife, Gene, and their daughter, Charlotte, onboard. Before Eddy and Al departed that day, Eddy called and asked me to meet them at Jet East. He gave me directions and said that he looked forward to seeing me there.

I went to the airport with my father and we waited at Jet East. For the next several years, I would be doing a lot of waiting at Jet East. I recognized Eddy's voice on the radio as he called ahead, "Jet East, Lear One Dallas Cowboys, we're about 20 minutes out. We'll be on the ramp for about four hours and then we'll be going back out. There should be two people there to meet us. Are they there?" he asked.

"Yes, they're here," she answered. When they taxied to the ramp at Jet East I had to pinch myself. The airplane had undergone a completely new paint and interior refurbishing since I had last seen it in Miami. It was officially Lear One Dallas Cowboys and I was officially standing there. As I walked out to greet everyone, I was so excited that I could hardly contain myself. Al went home to Little Rock. Eddy invited my father and I to lunch. It was several hours before departure.

Eddy informed me that I would fly an orientation flight to Austin with them that afternoon, we would return early that evening. I was scared and excited at the same time. Mike McCoy, the Cowboys Vice-President and minority partner, was onboard. He was Jerry's geologist and he also headed up Jerry's oil and gas operations in the United States and Canada. He and Jerry had been together for several years. Stephen Jones, Jerry's oldest son, was also a Cowboys Vice-President. He and Mike were flying together. I was surprised to learn that Stephen was only two years older than I was.

We departed Dallas and I was amazed. It was my first flight as an actual crew member of a jet airplane. I was overwhelmed at the complexity and the speed. I always thought that flying was flying but I had leaped from the aviation equivalent of pee-wee league to the Super Bowl. The speed, oh the speed, it was incredible. Things happened fast, real fast. My dad, a pilot for the past 30 years, went along with us. We flew them to Austin for a business meeting. We were to depart that evening and return to Dallas. I had all of my clothes packed for my stay at the Embassy Suites hotel near Simuflite's training center.

That 6:00 p.m. departure finally became a 1:00 a.m. departure when Stephen and Mike finally arrived. We flew back to Dallas, everyone deplaned, and I was in bed at 3:00 a.m. I had to be at Simuflite at 8:00 a.m. that morning. "Todd, how was your first day?" Stephen asked. "Long," I replied. Hindsight is 20/20 and that word would echo through my thoughts on a daily basis. I was 23 years old, and the experiences that would last a lifetime were set to begin.

I successfully completed my training and flew my first official flight on May 4, 1990. Eddy and I flew to Houston, Texas, with only Jerry onboard. On our return flight home that evening we were safely on our way when Jerry yelled to the cockpit, "Todd, come here, I want to talk to you for a minute." I was about to sit down for an informal meeting with the same person I had seen just last year pounding on podiums and spitting adjectives at 100 m.p.h.. My first thought was "What have I done?" As I nestled into the luxurious leather captain's chair to face him as he sat on the couch in the rear, Jerry said, "No, no, sit down beside me, right here." His bright blue eyes instantly mesmerized me as he motioned to the seat next to him.

Jerry began to tell me that life over the past 12 months had been pure hell. He had been in the middle of his worst nightmare and warned I would soon be in it too. It hadn't been all bad. Prior to my "heart-to-heart" conversation with him I remembered that he had handed out a then record six-year contract of $11.037 million to Heisman trophy winner Troy Aikman, the quarterback from U.C.L.A. He had also supported Jimmy Johnson in his selection of former pupil, and current Chicago Bear, Steve Walsh in the supplemental draft.

He helped orchestrate the trade of Herschel Walker to Minnesota, moved the Cowboys training camp site from Thousand Oaks, California, to Austin, and inducted the great, but spurned, Lee Roy Jordan into the exclusive "Ring of Honor" at Texas Stadium. He also helped negotiate a new pre-season TV contract, approved an aggressive plunge into the Plan B free agent market, built an indoor weight room at Valley Ranch and pushed for Paul Tagliabue as new NFL commissioner. In addition, he had given an inexperienced but highly touted college coach from the University of Miami, the head coaching job and the security of a 10-year contract.

Jerry lamented that it had been one hellacious rookie year, yet he seemed to take it all in stride. His tie was loosely tied and his shirt sleeves were rolled up as he sipped on a bourbon and Diet Coke. The "New Regime's" owner was real, personable, and accessible. As we talked he reminded me to call him Jerry. I realized that my preconceived notions of him were wrong—he really was a "people person." That is the single reason why I believe he became so successful. He was the master.

"Did you know that I paid over $140 million for the Cowboys and the lease to Texas Stadium? Many staff and administrative departments had to be reduced, but my flight crew is very, very important to me. I trust in Eddy, Al, and now you, to be there for me and to be the best. I'm demanding, I'm a workaholic, and if I have something on my mind I'll tell you," he said.

"There are a lot of things that I want to accomplish and you can help us do that. There will be many long days and many long nights, but I can't do it without you guys. Todd, can I count on you?" he asked. "Jerry, I wouldn't miss this for the world," I replied with a shy smile. "Okay, Okay," he said as he smiled broadly.

As I stood up to walk toward the front, he asked excitedly, "How does it feel to be a Dallas Cowboy?" It feels great," I replied proudly. "Yes it does, doesn't it?" he said, grinning. Always positive, upbeat, and enthusiastic, he was willing to push it to the limit and beyond. That was the first, and only time, Jerry Jones ever talked with me about the past.

A few days later we headed south. The entire Jones family was onboard. Jerry, his wife of 27 years, Gene, Stephen, their eldest son and Karen, his fiancee', Charlotte, their only daughter and her boyfriend, Shy, and Jerry, Jr. We flew to Destin, Florida, the "sunshine state" for a long weekend at the beach. I wasn't going to have any trouble keeping up with Jerry and the Joneses because as far as I was concerned, I was in heaven. My life was blue skies and tailwinds....

1

I LIKE MY #!+&+@ AIRPLANE!

Jerry Jones gained his experience in trading up for the NFL draft in 1987 when he began looking for a corporate jet. With the numerous oil and gas concerns that Jerry was engaged in, most notably The Arkoma Production Companies, Jerral W. Jones Oil and Gas, and JMC Exploration, his operations had outgrown the capabilities of his turboprop Beechcraft King Air 200. With oil and gas offices on the west coast and his expansion internationally into Calgary, time was money, and jet travel became inevitable.

The deciding factors were: Price–No more than $3 million. Performance–Must be able to get into and out of short runways and small airports. Cost of Operation-Flight Department and aircraft cost to operate and maintain. It came down to a decision between the Cessna Citation II or a Learjet 35A. Both fit the bill; both had advantages and disadvantages. Jerry liked the Citation and had set his mind to buying a new one.

The Lear was much more airplane for the money but Jerry had heard a few too many rumors about the "Fearjet." All that aside, I often wondered what happened to the Citation salesman who made the fatal mistake of telling Jerry Jones that he couldn't afford it. You don't tell the man he can't afford something. He can afford it. Period.

After careful consideration and consultation with Eddy, Jerry made the final decision. He decided to buy the Citation. He was hell bent to buy a new one right off the production line. Many times a company needed to move their purchase and/or date back for their new aircraft delivery. A person could switch places and trade up a spot. Although Jerry's delivery date was several months down the line, there was an airplane coming off the assembly line several spots ahead. It was available. Jerry traded up.

Just like he said about his total involvement in the daily operations of the Dallas Cowboys organization two years later, he was "socks to jocks" in the middle of handling all of the financial negotiations, as well as details for the airplane purchase. He took every recommendation and suggestion, analyzed them, and still remained firm with his original decision. Some things never changed, but it was his money.

Buying a corporate jet is similar to purchasing a new car. When ordering one directly from the factory, they will custom make it to each and every customer's personal taste—for a price. Jerry was making decisions and he told them exactly what he desired. He wanted this, and he wanted that. He wanted an interior with these amenities, and those accessories, etc. There was a difference between telling them what he wanted and having them ask why he wanted it. Never, never ask why! That was when the dumbest Citation salesman in the country asked, "You don't need that. Are you sure you want that? Can you afford that?"

Eddy said that Jerry reached into his coat pocket, found his checkbook, and wrote out a personal check for $1.8 million dollars! He handed it to the salesman. He also handed him some future business advice, "I don't want your airplane, but here is your money. Oh, one more thing, don't you ever, EVER, tell me that I can't afford something," he said as he stormed out. The salesman looked at him surprised and visibly shaken by the sudden outburst. Whether or not the money was returned, or his deposit ever refunded, I don't know. At that point it didn't matter anyway. Jerry bought the Learjet instead.

The initial expense of upgrades to the avionics and numerous modifications to the Lear quickly added up. When George Mitchell in Fort Smith, Arkansas, realized the astronomical amount of money required to operate and maintain the airplane...well. George was Jerry's head bean counter. He was in charge of the Flight Department budget, and every other budget for that matter. He advised Jerry to sell the airplane—immediately.

Jerry, Mike McCoy, George, the various oil and gas executives from Fort Smith and Little Rock, Arkansas, Oklahoma City, Oklahoma, Sacramento, California, and Calgary, Canada, convened and held their annual meetings in Little Rock. George probably hated paying the bills to maintain and fly the turboprop, much less a Learjet.

Accountants despised corporate aircraft. That's the difference between the people that "count" the money and the people that "make" the money. Jerry knew that

Jerry Jones and the "New Regime"

the Learjet had provided a full month of time saved in-flight over the King Air 200. Jerry Jones was the definition of "frequent flyer." That was a lot of time saved for anyone. Especially for a person that literally generated millions upon millions of dollars during the course of a two-minute telephone conversation. Enough said.

After all the department managers had presented their business statements on making the money, it was time for George to count the beans. "Jerry, you need to sell the airplane; it is a financial quagmire," George said. He continued on and on for no less than 15 minutes. He related the financial situation and gave his recommendations where needed savings would apply. He continued bellyaching about the cost of the Learjet.

Eddy, as Chief Pilot and Flight Department Manager, was probably sweating after sitting on the hot seat. In order to be a pilot, there had to be an airplane to fly. Eddy said that Jerry listened with intent. He pushed back his chair, stood up from the table, and walked to the front of the conference room where George was standing. Jerry put both hands on George's shoulders and looked him straight in the eyes. "George, I like my goddamn airplane. You just pay the bills," Jerry said. Then he turned around, walked back to his chair and sat down. Six years later, George Mitchell was still paying the bills, Jerry Jones was the owner of the Dallas Cowboys, and we were still flying the Learjet. Jerry always has, and always will, like his goddamn airplane.

George was exactly right about one thing. Maintaining any corporate aircraft is an evil necessity. It can be very, very expensive; but not too expensive for Jerry Jones. On the surface it seemed to be, with $40-50,000 per month in fuel cost alone. An average cost of nearly

I Like My #!+&+@ Airplane!

$1,200 per hour to operate and maintain. We were in the air a minimum of 20 days per month, and away from home more than that. Don't forget flight crew salaries, insurance, hotels and rental cars. The list of expenses was endless.

Like the old saying goes, "You need money to make money." A corporate flight department can cost a small fortune, especially when a Learjet was needed to keep up with the Joneses.

I know, and Jerry will agree, it's worth every penny.

2

LEAR 1 DC

I could hear them coming down the taxiway. For the first time I saw the airplane that looked like it was moving while sitting still. They turned onto the ramp at Jet East, taxied a few hundred feet and parked One Dallas Cowboys. Wearing gleaming white with long sweeping silver and blue stripes, sleek and long from her nose, across the fuselage and through her tail. Swoosh. A large Dallas Cowboys helmet was painted on the tail to let the world know. The sun was shining on that lovely lady, the sports car of business jets—a Learjet.

Suddenly, the door opened and Jerry Jones daughter, Charlotte, stepped out into the Dallas sun. Tall, statuesque and attractive. I remember thinking "Oh, Lord," as she walked toward the terminal. I was standing there with my father. I was in awe, in a blur, and my mind was racing. She was friendly and spoke, "Hi, how are you?" I replied, "Fine, I'm fine," I think. She had no idea who I was which just about made two of us.

Jerry Jones and the "New Regime"

The automatic doors at Jet East opened. I walked out onto the tarmac to greet the two men that I would be spending many of my days and nights with, Eddy Collins and Al Devens. They showed me the inside of my new home. It was luxurious: five silver-gray leather seats, faux marble cabinets, overhead recessed cabin lighting, light gray carpeting, a Dallas Cowboys helmet rug in front of the couch that could seat three comfortably in the very back, a flightphone, a programmable ten stack compact disc player and tables built into the walls that could be folded together to make a desk or area for eating. It also included a refreshment center and a fully stocked bar with bourbon, scotch, and vodka. Jerry Jones and up to seven others traveled in style.

I climbed over into the cockpit and seemed to become part of the airplane, molded into the front. Top of the line avionics, a global navigation system, a crew flight phone, intercom system, and sheepskin seat covers over custom seats for their pilots. It was everything I expected it to be and I hadn't even seen it at night yet. A Dallas Cowboys helmet was etched into the glass behind the co-pilot's seat. At night, with the lights shining on it, it was exquisite. Special flood lights were built into the exterior tail section designed to illuminate one of the most recognized insignias in professional sports: The Dallas Cowboys.

It was obvious that the helmet would make quite an impression taxiing down any runway. Keeping a low profile at destinations was not an easy task. Jerry Jones was not one to keep a low profile, why was I surprised? The airplane became very well-known throughout the entire United States. With unforgettable call letters, Lear One Dallas Cowboys, and that unmistakable logo, we always made an entrance and we always drew a crowd.

Eddy told me that although he and Jerry spent countless hours poring over every transformation detail, when they finally rolled her out for Jerry to see, as he admired her, he was overcome with emotion. Tears welled up in his blue eyes. I will never forget the feelings I had that sunny April afternoon in 1990 when I, too, saw her for the first time. Her proud logo glistening in the Dallas sun. The Dallas Cowboys. "America's Team." A Learjet.

She was, and still is, a beautiful lady.

3

I DID IT—MY WAY

Shortly after my arrival in Dallas in the spring of 1990, as people found out I was working for the Cowboys, I became a lightning rod for the storm that has never really ended. Intrigue and mystique aside, typical conversations were, "So, you work for that sorry mother?" "I wouldn't be tellin' that if I was you." "Every time he opens that hillbilly mouth of his it makes me wanna puke." "Redneck." "You workin' for the idiot that fired Tom!" Kind words were few and far between.

I really was not prepared for, and could not believe, the seemingly outright hatred that many people felt toward Jerry Jones. I thought I came into the picture after things were comfortable, however, things were not very comfortable in Dallas, Texas. I guess that 1-15 inaugural season didn't help very much. Naturally, I was curious so I asked Eddy, and eventually Jerry.

The Dallas Cowboys were on the market for the second time in four years. The working relationships between Tom Landry, Tex Schramm, and "Bum" Bright were not good. Apparently, Coach Landry did not know that the team was once again "For Sale." How could he have known? The three men who personified, who in essence were the Dallas Cowboys, were not even on speaking terms.

Fourteen or fifteen potential owners entered the bidding in the early spring of 1988 to purchase the Cowboys. The field quickly narrowed to three; a garment manufacturer from New York, a group of Japanese businessmen, and Jerral Wayne Jones from Little Rock, Arkansas. Try a life-sized picture of "America's Team" Japanese owned. Try Japanese coached!

Jerry reached an agreement with "Bum" Bright on February 25, 1989. The NFL owners called a special meeting in New York City on April 18, 1989, where they unanimously voted to approve Jerry. Two solid months of long days and sleepless nights had been the order of the day. The Learjet, and its out-of-control new owner, flew over 150 hours per month. The days of ducking and running had begun.

With the media blitz on, Eddy told me it was a nightmare. They literally hit all four corners of the United States in a 24-hour period. They flew everywhere to pick up and drop off, filing no flight plans until airborne, as they tried desperately to keep away from all of the news media and their helicopters.

At the tainted coaxing of Tex Schramm, Eddy flew the infamous flight to Austin's Lakeway Airpark, Tom Landry's home. As Jerry and Tex arrived, we can only imagine how Tom must have felt. He probably had his suspicions but he could not have been prepared for, "I'm Jerry Jones. I'm the new owner of the Dallas Cowboys, and you have two options." Good evening to you too, sir.

The only head coach in the 29-year history of "God's Team," the Dallas Cowboys, was unceremoniously placed on waivers. Tom Landry was not fired, he was simply "allowed" to retire. Jerry continued and promised, "I will honor your contract in full, the $1 million dollars that you are due, is yours. But, University of Miami's Jimmy Johnson is and will be my new Head Coach."

Jerry offered a little-known second option. "You can work in player personnel, you can work anywhere you see fit in the Cowboys front offices." Tom Landry—the stoic keeper of the Cowboys fold, the same man that was third on the NFL's all-time win list with 250 career victories, the father of five NFC champions, 13 division champions, two Super Bowl championships and 20 consecutive winning seasons from 1966-1985, was abruptly shown the exit sign of the "New Regime's" revolving door.

Tom Landry, the epitome of Dallas Cowboys football had left an indelible mark. He exercised his thinly veiled but only real option, he took the money and stepped aside. Of course, we now know that his departure was not the quiet one that Jerral Wayne had hoped for. If only it could have been that simple.

Jerry, always impatient and blinded by all of the excitement, failed to realize the consequences of his freshman apprenticeship. In the conservative annals of Dallas Cowboys football, each and every one of those incidents were nothing short of monumental.

Jerry said, "The real problem was, we rolled three life-changing major events all into one. The ownership change, the management and coaching change, and the hiring of Jimmy. It made me look like I lacked sensitivity or any appreciation for the past. "Bum" offered to handle the situation but I felt I had to stand up like a man. I felt I had to do it...." If I had it to do all over again, I would have spread it out. I would have purchased the team by itself. Then I could have hired Jimmy and done the other 'things' at a later time. Instead, there was this big press conference, it went terrible, and the shit hit the fan...." That was as close to the truth as I came and it remained my patent answer to the faithful.

It was out with the "old" and in with the "new." Precious few emerged unscathed, the least of which was Jerry himself. Twenty-four hour guards, due to numerous bomb and death threats, were placed on the Learjet. It might as well have been "arms for hostages," but it wasn't. It was simply the first of many hard days on the job for only the third owner in Dallas Cowboys history.

The sad truth is, I vividly experienced most of the tireless hatred first-hand, and on a nationwide basis. Jerry often chose to arrive very late at night so as not to awaken any sleeping enemies. I defended Jerry no less than a million times because I know the man. I defended him not because he signed my paychecks. I defended him for one reason and one reason only. I know that after 29 years it didn't really matter who purchased "America's Team," the beloved Dallas Cowboys.

They wouldn't have liked you either....

4

THE HOLDOUTS

Jerry Jones seemed to always get what he wanted. Sometimes it just took him longer than he liked. When he first purchased the Cowboys from H.R. "Bum" Bright, the majority owner in 1989, there were several other minority owners. Little pieces of "America's Team" that others besides Jerry owned. How could Jerry be in 100% complete and total control of the situation if he wasn't 100% owner?

He would have none of that. He slowly and methodically worked his magic all the way toward the last holdouts, Ed and Mollie Smith. A group headed by Arthur Temple of Tyler, Texas, and Ed were the only remaining minority owners of the Cowboys. Jerry was frustrated over the stalemate in his constant negotiations concerning Ed Smith's 27% stake in "Jerry's Team."

Unbeknownst to Ed and Mollie, they gave Jerry fits. One of the very first flights I ever flew in Lear One Dallas Cowboys was to pick them up in Houston, where they lived. We flew to Houston and brought them back to Dallas for many of the Cowboys home games, then we took them home afterwards. Jerry tried his best to salt the cow to get the calf.

Jerry acted like he loved them. He played the part with them. He endeared them to him. He was the proverbial "snake with a smile." Ed Smith had been an instrumental piece of the Bright/Jones purchase puzzle. That wasn't good enough. Jerry simply wanted as few as possible holdovers from the past. He would gladly take all of the tradition and grandeur of Dallas Cowboys football. But, the "New Regime" was to be all his alone. ALONE!

I quickly learned that many of the staffers at Valley Ranch, and several employees at Texas Stadium Corporation, didn't trust Jerry. Everyone was a little wary. I was beginning to see the reasons why. It was a rare and pleasant surprise for many Cowboys employees whenever Jerry backed himself into a corner. They didn't realize that every move was calculated, weighed, and masterfully orchestrated.

We flew the Smiths many, many times during their holdout. I always assumed they simply upped their price until it suited them, just like another Smith we all know. Jerry played his patent hard ball, but if the end justified the means, then he would compromise. Only if and when he had to. If your last name is Smith, watch out when dealing with Jones!

Ed and Mollie Smith were good people. They were the nicest couple that we flew but Jerry seemed to despise them. One year Gene won a very special award of her own. She was named "Mother of the Year" in Little Rock. She probably won for putting up with

The Holdouts

Jerry. For Gene's celebrity "roast," Eddy and I flew to Houston and picked up the Smiths. We flew back through Dallas and met Mike McCoy, Jimmy Johnson, and other guests for the flight to the Jones' hometown.

It was a much bigger event than I thought and a virtual "Who's Who" of Dallas socialites. It was also a very busy day and night afterwards for the flight crew. Dallas oilman, T. Boone Pickens, flew his private Falcon Jet to Little Rock for the festivities, also. He had Troy Aikman, Michael Irvin and several others onboard. Gene definitely deserved the honor and everyone enjoyed the gala.

Before we departed Jet East that evening, I was standing in the lobby waiting and talking with Jimmy Johnson and the Smiths. Mike McCoy walked over, "Todd, are we going to have any champagne and food on the flight?" he asked. "Yes, Mike, Dom Perignon, finger sandwiches and a cheese platter," I replied. "Oh, then it's the usual?" he replied and then sauntered away.

Everyone looked at me dumbfounded. They couldn't believe that Dom Perignon was "the usual." Mike and I laughed about that for a long time. It became an inside joke because unless we were smoozin' and scratchin' we never had more than snacks onboard the airplane. "The usual" was usually a cup of coffee. Jerry did his best to impress them that day, though. Eventually, as always, he was victorious in his quest.

There would be many casualties over the next several years, most notably Jimmy Johnson. The Smiths were unfortunately one of the first to buckle under the incessant pressure of the one thing that Jerry Jones demanded the most—100% control. CONTROL!

He just never liked holdouts. Especially if their last name was Smith. Just ask Emmitt!

5

BORN TO FLY

Have you ever walked out into the parking lot at the mall and forgotten where you parked the car? After a frantic search and still no car, did you think "My car has been stolen" and then you found it? It happened to Jerry Jones, too.

The only difference was that Jerry Jones was in and out of a numerous and wide variety of rental, courtesy, and sponsor-provided automobiles during the course of his day. This particular time it was the parking lot at Alamo Stadium in San Antonio, Texas.

Since San Antonio did not have a professional football team, it was decided that the annual Texas Governor's Cup scrimmage would be played in San Antonio on Saturday, July 28, 1990. The Cowboys scrimmaged their interstate rivals, the Houston Oilers, on neutral turf.

The game served as a pre-season tune up for the third week of practices. The players and coaching staff

Jerry Jones and the "New Regime"

rode on chartered buses from Austin to San Antonio. Everyone else drove the 70 miles or so in their own cars.

Not the Joneses. Jerry and Gene took Lear One Dallas Cowboys for the 15-minute flight. Really it was more like an 8,000 foot hop. At our normal cruise speed the Lear would only take about eight minutes to cover the distance. It really was more trouble for them to drive to the Austin Airport, park their car, get out and through the Page AvJet terminal, get on the airplane, takeoff, hop, land, taxi to parking, get in their rental car, and make it to the game. That was much easier than if they had just driven in the first place, right? Not for Jerry, and certainly not for Gene. After all, we once flew Gene from Dallas to Little Rock to get her hair done.

We always had all of the company credit cards, so Eddy placed the charge for Jerry's luxury rental car on his credit card. Jerry sped away with Gene. Eddy and I borrowed a courtesy car from Fairchild Gen Aero and we drove to the stadium.

In the middle of the fourth quarter, Eddy and I were prepared to leave the game early so that we could get a jump on traffic. That gave us plenty of time to make sure we were ready to go when Jerry and Gene arrived. As we left the suite, we spotted Jerry coming down the hallway. "What time do you think you'll be at the airport?" we asked. "Oh, I'll be there within the hour," Jerry replied.

It was just a scrimmage, but it was the first time the coaches were given an opportunity to see their first glimpse of the pivotal 1990 Cowboys butt heads with someone besides Jimmy Johnson. Starting quarterback Troy Aikman hit 7 of 11 passes for 77 yards, Steve Walsh went 9 of 16 for 137 yards and a touchdown. Third string QB, Babe Laufenberg, took the team in for the tying score.

Jimmy was pleased with the aggressive play of Dave Wannstedt's defense. Jerry commented several times that "We look good, we look good...."

Set and ready to go, Eddy and I waited...and waited...and waited. Jerry and Gene were an hour late...then two hours late...then two and a half hours late. We had just seen him; it wasn't like we had not been in contact with him for a day or two. He WAS there, but now he wasn't. Jerry Jones was not exactly the most popular guy in Texas in the summer of 1990. He had been loudly booed after being pointed out to the crowd by the game's announcer.

I was in Booth 4D with Gene and the others when that very public display of fan resentment was displayed. A pained expression came over Gene's beautiful face; she buried her face in her hands. "God, will it ever end?" she wondered aloud. Jerry was standing inconspicuously in his now familiar sideline pose during the game. For that reason, I began to worry. What if something had happened to him?

They may have hated the owner, but that game proved to me the Cowboys really were "America's Team." Nearly 14,000 fans paid admission to Alamo Stadium to watch a 24-24 tie between the Cowboys and Oilers. I overheard a fan in the parking lot on the way in say he had driven over 500 miles to see the Cowboys—500 miles to watch a scrimmage! Meanwhile....

Had the car been stolen? If it was, I was thankful it was on Eddy's credit card and not mine. It made sense. Jerry was the kind of guy who always left his car keys over the visor or dangling in the ignition. There were not enough seconds in his busy schedule for car keys.

Naturally, it could have been stolen right out of the parking lot of Alamo Stadium.

Eventually, Jerry and Gene drove up, three hours later. He was flabbergasted. It must have been quite a sight to see him walking around the stadium's parking lot trying to find their "unknown" car. It had to be difficult for him to find it when he could not remember what kind of car he had driven to the game, much less the color. Jerry waited until everyone had left and the parking lot was virtually empty before he found the rental car.

At first he figured, "I must have parked it somewhere else." On second thought, some people were just born to fly.

6

JETHRO HAD TO GO!

My first encounter with anyone other than the "New Regime" was the August 3, 1990, Hall of Fame flight to the Akron Canton Regional Airport in Canton, Ohio. Coach Tom Landry was inducted into the Pro Football Hall of Fame in his first year of eligibility...and rightly so. Jerry made sure that the Cowboys arrived in style. He made his private Learjet available to distinguished members of the "Old Guard." Drew Pearson, Robert Newhouse, Ed "Too Tall" Jones, Dick Nolan and Jethro Pugh (affectionately nicknamed Jethro Pugh-eee after the trip).

Roger Staubach was supposed to be onboard the flight, but due to prior commitments and scheduling conflicts, he flew via the airlines. Although an open-invitation was extended, Coach Landry elected not to ride Lear One Dallas Cowboys and Jerry elected not to attend the ceremonies. Imagine that.

That was my first real taste of the NFL. Parties at every major hotel lasted into the wee hours of the morning. There were exclusive invitation-only special events all around "Cooperstown" that weekend. Present and former NFL "greats" were everywhere. Mildly put, it was a rousing weekend for a small town Georgia boy who grew up with model airplanes hanging from his bedroom ceiling. My heroes really had always been Cowboys! I can remember telling my little brothers I was going to "Martinize" them, just like Harvey Martin, as I tackled them during our sibling football rivalries. Lord, I was in some mighty tall cotton.

On Saturday, August 4, the Festival Grand Parade began around 7:30 a.m. The actual enshrinement at the Hall of Fame Museum was scheduled for 10:00 a.m. Cowboys legend, Roger Staubach, presented Coach Landry with professional football's highest honor. Six other notables were also inducted that day. Buck Buchanan, Bob Griese, Franco Harris, Ted Hendricks, Jack Lambert and Bob St. Clair joined a very exclusive list. The Cowboys definitely showed their support for Coach Landry. Ten former players and coaches, including Bob Breunig and Bob Lilly, were in attendance.

After the induction ceremonies were over, Eddy and I met that very special group at the airport early Saturday afternoon for our flight back to Dallas. Prior to departure, Eddy made a point to encourage each and every one of them to use the "little boy's room." Although there was a small potty in the airplane, it was not exactly suitable for certain "things." We had at least a two and a half hour flight and they were drinking beer. No problem.

Jethro Had To Go!

Everyone was set and ready to go. Remember seeing stuffed grizzly bears in a museum? Imagine trying to load several of them into an 11'x5'x4' tube. I never realized how big they were until I saw them piling into the back. They maneuvered their big bodies into the Lear, continued drinking beer, and began playing cards. We had a plane full of fellas.

We taxied toward designated Runway 23 for departure. With all of the before takeoff checklists completed, the tower cleared us in position to hold for takeoff. Suddenly, from the rear of the airplane a grizzly growled, "Hold it!" Jethro had to go. Everyone in the back was laughing and making fun of him, but Jethro had to go! Now!

"Regional Tower this is Lear One Dallas Cowboys. We're going to need a back taxi to the terminal at this time," I requested. We taxied all the way back to the terminal at Wings, Inc. Jethro bolted toward the door with enough speed that I swear he could probably still play. He took off to take a shit. It took him awhile, but about 30 minutes later he reappeared, smiling. We reloaded the legends back into the Lear and headed for "Big D."

Coach Tom Landry never changed. He said all the right things and he thanked all the right people. He had been "fired" and inducted into The Pro Football Hall of Fame all in one year. I had experienced "Pro Football's Greatest Weekend" first hand. The only thing that sticks out in my mind, aside from the obvious, was the particulars of the ribbing that Jethro Pugh took on the flight back to Dallas that sunny August afternoon. There was never a dull moment.

Suffice it to say, he earned his nickname...Jethro Pugh-eee.

7

IS THAT LAKE MEAD?

Marylyn Love was Jerry Jones long-suffering personal secretary. If I ever needed to get in touch with Jerry at the Cowboys Valley Ranch headquarters, I had to go through Marylyn first. Bless her sweet heart, she did an admirable job of trying to keep the flight crew "scheduled."

Coordination of a flight crew, with a man that told time by a calendar, was not an easy task for her or us. Sometimes, we were lucky enough to know where the Joneses were supposed to go. Once in a "blue moon" we even had a fair idea when. Not this time.

In 1990, during the Cowboys training camp in Austin, everyone was looking forward to a much needed improvement over their 1989 1-15 season fiasco. The Cowboys were set and ready to begin their pre-season schedule. We were to depart Dallas on Friday and fly to San Diego, California, for pre-season game #1 on Saturday, August 11, against the Chargers. We would then remain on the west coast during the following week for the team to continue practice at the

Jerry Jones and the "New Regime"

University of California at San Diego. We would travel along the coast the following Friday for pre-season game #2, Saturday, August 18, against the Raiders in the L.A. Coliseum.

As usual, Jerry was running late when we finally departed Dallas that Friday afternoon. Jerry, Gene, Stephen, Karen, Charlotte, Jerry, Jr. and Mike McCoy were onboard. After an uneventful three-hour flight, Eddy and I were on approach to Runway 9 at San Diego's Lindbergh Field. We were in the middle of my first training camp, we had been busy. I was tired and looking forward to a few days of relaxation in sunny southern California.

The conversation was lively in the back of the airplane as they began to chatter about the big lake they were seeing out of Lear One Dallas Cowboys windows. "What lake is that?" I heard from the back. "That's Lake Mead." Eddy looked at me; I looked at him. Hmmmm. "I never realized it was that big...it's huge." We both heard that.

Now, if we had been flying a group of people who didn't know where in the hell Lake Mead was, I would not have been concerned. But one place that Jerry Jones was intimately familiar with was Las Vegas. We weren't anywhere near Las Vegas; we weren't anywhere near Lake Mead. That was not Lake Mead. It was, however, the Pacific Ocean.

Talk about effective communication and organization. Land o' Goshun! Someone had crossed some very big wires somewhere. We had known about this "scheduled" flight for several days. We had filed a flight plan. Even the often frazzled Marylyn did not know of the change in plans when we called her in Dallas. They wanted to go, and thought they were going, to Las Vegas for the evening, then on to San Diego the next day. That was the first time the flight crew had heard about it.

Eddy and I made the smoothest landing and taxied to the ramp at JimsAir. We parked, refueled, filed a new flight plan, laughed, and headed for...viva, Las Vegas. If traveling by air, it sometimes helped if the pilots were planning on flying to the same destination as the passengers. I still laugh when I think about the scientists in the back asking: "Is that Lake Mead?" Sure it was.

It really was amazing to me that an organization that has enjoyed such tremendous success would be as unorganized as they were. Marylyn told me the reason that the flight crew could not keep any semblance of a schedule, much less have any idea of when, what time, how long, or even our ultimate destination, was because the Joneses never knew themselves, until the very last minute, what they were going to do.

Even then, there was no guarantee of where we might have ended up because they often changed their minds during midflight. A simple one day flight to Little Rock often turned into a week and a half on the road, with stops in Florida and Canada along the way. We just never knew. I learned real quick to pack for a minimum of two weeks. Especially, if we were only "supposed to" be flying for the day.

It reminds me of the time Jerry and Gene were in the back of the airplane and in the mood to visit some friends. They were leafing through a Captains Atlas in midflight on their way to nowhere. Gene yelled to the cockpit, "Al, is Albuquerque on the way?" Al said, "Yeah." Then he turned, looked to me and asked, "On the way to where?" I just shrugged. Who knew?

There was one thing that we always knew. Regardless of the route that we took or didn't take, keeping up with the Joneses was an impossible task. Unbeknownst to their flight crew, and always subject to change, they were always going somewhere. They went at all hours of the day and night. Occasionally, they even let their pilots know where they wanted to go.

By the way, we didn't go to Albuquerque.

8

THE TROUBLE MAKER

Jesse Solomon was a heavy hitter and a hard player. He arrived in the fall of 1989 via the infamous Herschel Walker trade. Eddy and I departed Little Rock on August 25, 1990, flew to Tallahassee, Florida, and returned to Dallas with Jesse onboard. On the return flight that night, after a stop in Atlanta at Dekalb-Peachtree Airport, he was alone in the back of the Lear.

"Why don't you guys show me what this Lear can do?" Jesse asked. We did a high performance takeoff and it scared him. I think he had all he wanted of what Lear One Dallas Cowboys could do. Eventually, he had all he wanted of what Jerry Jones could do, too.

His fate was sealed. He was pegged as a troublemaker. It seems he had publicly bad-mouthed the Cowboys organization and Jerry as well. Jesse was a vocal personality and he let his feelings be known to anyone and everyone in the Dallas media that would listen. Jesse was unhappy about the trade with

Jerry Jones and the "New Regime"

Minnesota almost a year earlier. His meetings with Jerry obviously did not go as planned. He sat out the first seven games of the 1990 season due to a contract dispute. Jerry demanded respect regardless of personal feelings, and if one thought otherwise, they were well served to keep those feelings to themselves.

In March of 1991, I went home to Georgia for personal reasons. I flew via Delta Airlines to Atlanta, spent some time at home, and headed back to Dallas on Sunday evening. I was in my seat moments before departure and who boarded the airplane with a seat right next to mine? Jesse Solomon. He had been home to Tallahassee and was changing planes for the connecting flight to Dallas. Everyone knows their flights always connect in Atlanta.

"What are you doing, do you remember me, how come you're not flying private?" he asked. Jesse and I exchanged greetings and small talked. I could tell right away that it was going to be an interesting flight home to Dallas. I always liked talking and listening to the players. They always had a lot to say.

Since I was an integral part of the flight crew that flew Jerry all over the country, everyone always liked to ask me questions. I had been well versed on Jesse in the past, but now he began to talk about Jerry. Jesse felt like he had never received fair negotiations with the Cowboys. He knew that he had arrived in Dallas under strange circumstances, but he felt very strongly that Jerry and the Cowboys organization had been very adversarial in their contract talks with him.

I was defending Jerry, as always. Jesse was, well, I hate to use the word "racist" but maybe I will. Jesse stated that he felt the black players, during their contract negotiations did not get the same respect, treatment and consideration as did the white players.

Then he asked me, "Todd, do you fly any black players? Have you ever flown any black players?" I knew that we had flown several current and former Cowboys players, white and black. "Jesse, I have flown Drew Pearson, Robert Newhouse, Jethro Pugh, and 'Too Tall' Jones. I have also flown Alexander Wright and Emmitt Smith to name a few. Jesse, I have flown YOU!" I told him.

They were all business related trips. With Jerry Jones it was always business…everyday. It didn't matter if the player was white or black.

Only one color ever concerned Jerry—GREEN.

9

NUMBER 22

He was standing outside the terminal of the Pensacola Regional Airport facing the taxiway. He had a bag in each hand. Chomping at the bit he was, with his Mom and Dad standing beside him. He was a young man not even out of college. Maybe he was thinking the same thoughts I had the first time I saw Lear One Dallas Cowboys taxiing up the tarmac. He did not look like the perennial National Football League rushing champ then. I remember shaking his hand and introducing myself to Emmitt Smith.

It was September 4, 1990, when Eddy and I received the urgent call. We went to the airport immediately and took off for Atlanta. We flew to Dekalb-Peachtree Airport and picked up his agents, Richard Howell and Pat Dye, Jr. We then flew to Pensacola, Florida, and brought Emmitt Smith home to Dallas.

I grew up in Georgia and The University of Georgia was less than one hour away. I knew why Emmitt was the Cowboys #1 draft pick. The entire

Jerry Jones and the "New Regime"

Southeastern Conference, and most certainly the Georgia Bulldogs, breathed a huge sigh of relief. I was one of the first Cowboys employees to meet and greet him. "Damn, I'm glad you're here. I'm from Georgia and I know the Bulldogs are glad you're here, too," I said. We have been friends ever since.

Emmitt was the youngest football player at that time ever to sign a professional contract. Jerry had been playing hard ball economics and would not sign him. Emmitt knew his worth and played some hard ball of his own...he held out for the duration of training camp and the pre-season. The powers that be had finally agreed to terms, and as they say, "the rest is history."

Jerry and Mike McCoy were at the airport to greet him in person when he stepped off the airplane. A few quick handshakes and they whisked him through the Jet East lobby and straight upstairs to the conference room. He signed on the spot. They wanted to make sure it was a done deal.

Despite missing training camp and the pre-season in 1990, Emmitt went on to become the unanimous choice as NFL Offensive Rookie of the Year, voted in by every major news wire and sports publication in the country. He then became the first Cowboys player to participate in the Pro Bowl since 1988. In 1991, he became the first Cowboy ever to lead the league in rushing. Following the 1992 and 1993 seasons, his NFL rushing titles totaled three. He owns two Super Bowl rings, one league M.V.P., and he was the 1993 Super Bowl M.V.P. His first five seasons have also produced five Pro Bowl honors and 7,183 rushing yards. Emmitt knew his worth alright.

It seems like yesterday when Eddy and I taxied up to the terminal in Pensacola. I can still see him standing there. Come to think of it, I may be the only person who has ever seen him standing still since that day.

Not long ago I ran into Emmitt at, of all places, the local dry cleaners in Valley Ranch. "Hey, Todd, you still flying those planes?" he asked. "I still am, just not for the Cowboys," I replied. "Man, it's good to see you, been awhile, how are you?" I asked.

As we continued to chat, a crowd instantly started to form. A little Cowboy fan walked up with a scratch pad and a pen. Emmitt signed the autograph, then he tore off an extra sheet. He wrote his new home phone number down and handed it to me. "It's good to see you Todd, take care. Give me a call," he said.

With the national headlines constantly focused around America's love affair with their gridiron super heroes, rest assured, for all his success, glory, and personal achievement, number 22 is a team player, not a *me* player. Emmitt knows that everybody comes from somewhere and it was always best not to forget where.

Emmitt J. Smith III is one of the nicest people I have ever met.

10

TIME FLIES

    The once proud Dallas Cowboys were a thing of the past when I arrived in Dallas. The jokes about the Cowboys from their "fair weather fans" were abundant. Without a winning season since 1985 they were still "America's Team," but a lot of people had forgotten. The jokes were plentiful and the fans always had their latest to tell me. Jerry Jones was fair game and everyone knew it.
    I was sitting in a Dallas bar and grille with several of my friends. It didn't seem to take very long to make friends with a Cowboys business card in my pocket. We were sitting there when one of one of my new friends spotted an old friend of his across the bar. He was headed our way. Evidently, that infamous Herschel Walker trade was still etched in everyone's mind. They tried desperately to erase Jerry and his college friend, Jimmy, out of their minds, too, it seemed.
    He walked over, sat down with us, and introduced himself to me. He did not know that I

Jerry Jones and the "New Regime"

worked for the Cowboys. "Hey, I heard that the Cowboys were for sale," he said. Everyone knew that Jerry had just purchased them a little over a year ago, but after that 1-15 season, maybe they were hoping that this was not a joke. Maybe the man who fired their beloved "man in the hat" had seen the light. Maybe he had decided to go home to Arkansas. Not a chance.

Altogether the fans chimed in with "You're kidding!" They were still unaware that it was a joke. Half of them listened in disbelief, the others were in anxious prayer. I just listened; I knew better. "Nope, I heard on the news tonight that the Cowboys were for sale," he replied. No one really seemed to believe him. "Yeah, they are. They said that the Ringling Brothers and Barnum and Bailey Circus wants to buy them," he continued.

"What do you mean?" they asked. Everyone was curious. "Why would a circus want to buy the Cowboys?" one of them asked. "Well, they don't want the football team, they just want the two clowns that are running it," he replied. Everyone burst out laughing, it was funny. Imagine his surprise when they told him who I was. I spent a lot of my time defending Jerry Jones. He knew that all "they" wanted was a winner. He did everything in his power to provide them with one. Jerry believed everything would be fixed with success. He was partially right.

The Cowboys record improved dramatically during the course of the 1990 season. Things had changed, but they weren't quite there yet. In January, everyone started planning their Super Bowl parties, even though the Cowboys season had ended a month earlier. My friends asked me what I was going to do for the Super Bowl. I knew I was going to be in attendance. I told them the same thing that Jerry told me.

"We go to the Super Bowl every year...we just don't take the team." Time flies doesn't it?

11

EVERY CITY LOOKS THE SAME

It was the beginning of the end. Even though Al was slightly older than Eddy, he always liked to go and see the sights. But not Eddy. Whenever I flew with Al we ventured out into the city and left the hotel far behind. Lear One Dallas Cowboys flew all over the United States, the Virgin Islands, Mexico and Canada. We always needed to unwind and relax. Al and I agreed that from a hotel room every city looked exactly the same.

Eddy often reminded me of a joke that my dad used to tell me. It was about an airline captain, the co-pilot and their flight engineer. My dad was the reason I had become a pilot in the first place. I was bitten by the aviation bug at a very early age. Every pilot will agree that flying gets in your blood, it becomes a way of life. My dad had been an airline pilot for 25 years. He always knew exactly what I was talking about—good, bad or ugly.

These days, most jet airplanes operate with two-man flight crews. It was not always that way. In the supposedly good 'ol days, they flew with three-man crews. Whenever they arrived in some far away and exotic location, they checked into the hotel. No matter how long the day had been, it was always the same. The young flight engineer ran to his room, showered, and went to the hotel bar. He wanted to check out the ladies.

The middle-aged co-pilot went to his room and promptly called home. He spent 30 minutes talking to his wife, daughter and son. Then he watched the news, took a shower, and went to bed. He had comfortably settled into life, living out of his suitcase. It was important that he kept his family values.

The old and experienced captain had seen it all before, many, many times. He walked into the hotel room and threw his bags on the floor. He promptly headed for the bathroom, sat down, and took a shit. Then he went straight to bed. The bathroom was top priority. It takes a very special person to fly airplanes for a living. It also takes a very understanding and supportive family at home. Even so, I would not trade any of my experiences for the world.

With the schedule that we kept, however, I became a "captain" long before my time.

12

A DUMB...SMART ASS

There is no denying the fact that during the "New Regime's" Super Bowl runs, the Dallas Cowboys had arguably one of the best coaching staffs in the National Football League. With head motivator Jimmy Johnson as the real driving force, the entire organization overcame all odds and became The Best. Among the best were Dave Wannstedt's hard-hitting defense and Tony Wise's All-Pro offensive line. Add Norv Turner, the offensive "boy wonder," and this was truly a highly talented and devoted group. Successful people surround themselves with other successful people, and few can question their accomplishments.

However, would you believe that all of the coaches were not exactly bright? There has to be one in every group. Who would that be? How about Mr. Personality himself—strength and conditioning coach, Mike Woicik. Whether lifting weights or running, his involvement with the Cowboys players certainly contributed to the team's success. The Cowboys weight and

Jerry Jones and the "New Regime"

training room at the club's Valley Ranch headquarters was his office. I hear he's also an excellent bowler. It figured.

With most of my time spent away from home, if I was not exhausted, I worked out, maybe swam a few laps at the hotel pool or played tennis with Eddy. It was a great stress reliever.

During an away game in the New Jersey Meadowlands, the assistant coaches and select staff, including myself, hurriedly filed their way back into their seats in the visiting coaches booth after halftime meetings.

I had tried for some time to gain a few extra pounds. Who better to ask some quick weight and health-related questions than the man in charge of keeping all of your Dallas Cowboys favorites mean and sometimes even lean? It was a simple question or two. Or so I thought.

"Coach Woicik, how do the players keep and put on all their weight and bulk?" I asked. "Huh?" That was not exactly the reply I had in mind. "I'd like to put on about 15-20 pounds and I was wondering if there is a special diet or weight program you could recommend to help me gain a few pounds. What can I do?" I asked again. "Well, first of all you're going to have to speak up because I'm deaf in my left ear. Secondly, eat!" he replied.

That was it? All the helpful advice I could muster was that I needed to eat! What a tremendous help he was. I still don't like him—what an asshole. I, however, do have some helpful advice for Mike.

"Deaf, dumb and ugly is no way to go through life!"

13

CROSSING THE LINE

For some reason the Arizona Cardinals have always played the Cowboys tough. We should beat the stuffing out of those birds. Every time we played them, however, the final score would be low. After the October 14, 1990, game in Phoenix, which the Cowboys lost 20-3, Jerry was ready to beat the stuffing out of his own team. That was when he started crossing the line.

After his purchase of the Dallas Cowboys in 1989, Jerry Jones had undergone scrutiny normally reserved for someone with an FBI number. With most of his public relations faux pas now far behind him, "America's Team" was on the brink of an unexpected and dramatic turnaround. Jerry was in the spotlight and he started to like it.

Seldom, if ever, until the 1993 season, did Jerry and the Joneses ever fly with the coaches, players and news media on the American Airlines charters to away games. They always flew privately in Lear One Dallas Cowboys for a myriad of reasons.

Many times it depended upon scheduling. The charter always departed Saturday around 10:00 a.m. The team was required to be in the visiting city at least 24 hours prior to kick off. The football team was expected to perform one day per week. If only the flight crew could have been so lucky.

For example, if the Cowboys played on the west coast, we flew to Calgary and Sacramento for oil and gas meetings. Then, we stopped off in Las Vegas for a day or night. When Jerry, Jr. was in college at Georgetown, we flew into Washington, D.C. two or three days prior to the game at RFK so they could spend some time with him. We sometimes arrived in New York three or four days before the game so Gene could shop 'til she dropped.

After that particular Cardinals game, Jerry did not fly with the rest of the family through Little Rock and home to Dallas. Instead, he flew with the team on their charter home. I heard through the grapevine the following day that he was up and down the aisles of the 727 in everyone's face.

That type of tantrum was normally reserved, and reported on the following day, for Head Coach Jimmy Johnson. Jimmy's private life, thoughts, actions and activities were routinely dramatized in the Dallas media. Wisely, not one reporter exposed Jerry's temper.

I had only been associated with Jerry for six months at that time. His business decisions, comments and continuous intrusions were documented. No one ever seemed to question Jerry about much else. Personal questions were always answered vaguely unless it was something that he wanted to become public knowledge. Temper or no temper, Jimmy Johnson never enjoyed that privilege.

Jimmy and the team were upset to begin with. They knew they had given a poor account of themselves. But there was Jerry ranting, "I pay your check. You play for Jimmy, you work for ME! If you can't produce..." and so on. Apparently, his outbursts became real nasty, real quick.

For over two hours I was told he went up and down the aisles of the charter like he was holding a business meeting, or had just drilled a "dry hole." It started a ripple effect and the players began to break ranks. Tempers had begun to flare. That "gray area" in the Cowboys organization was now grayer than ever.

In every NFL franchise, the owner paid the bills, the coaches coached, and the players played. Jerry had stepped out of bounds and started a brawl. In his quest for complete and total control he had crossed the line. He committed a personal foul for unsportsmanlike conduct against everyone.

It didn't stop there, either. I heard he even fired a few janitors at Valley Ranch on Monday morning. He always did what he wanted to do. He always has and he always will. He has consistently proved that theory from day one. Quite possibly even today....

Can't teach new Cowboys, or old dogs, new tricks.

14

THE CONTRAIL

A Contrail, the visible white trail an airplane leaves behind, is as ephemeral as glory and just as thrilling to experience. Jerry Jones buys the glory, and one particular blue sky day, he bought a contrail.

We had arrived at our cruising altitude of 35,000 feet for our flight on October 16, 1990, from Dallas to Chicago's O'Hare International Airport for the NFL owners' annual fall meetings. Jerry made it a practice never to conduct important business over the air phone, so he was quietly perusing his notes in preparation for the next several days of meetings.

I checked in with Memphis Center. "Memphis Center, Lear One Dallas Cowboys, flight level three-five-zero," I said. "Lear One Dallas Cowboys, Memphis Center, roger, flight level three-five-zero," he replied. About 15 minutes later, still at normal cruise, Eddy and I were admiring the view from, in my biased opinion, the best seat in the house. Center called: "Lear One Dallas Cowboys, traffic at two o'clock, eight miles,

Jerry Jones and the "New Regime"

Southwest bound, flight level three-three-zero, a Boeing 737." I responded with "Lear One Dallas Cowboys...looking." Scanning the skies, we spotted our approaching traffic immediately to our right at the required 2,000 foot spacing below us, leaving a beautiful contrail in the October morning sky.

Jerry must have looked out the window at precisely that moment. Was it the graffiti writing kid in all of us, or was it the brash new NFL owner determined to leave his mark who called to us in the front and asked, "Can we make a 360?"

"A 360?" I asked. "Yes, a 360 degree turn," he confirmed. Whatever...I thought. "Hello Memphis, Lear One Dallas Cowboys, I have a request," I reluctantly said. "Lear One Dallas Cowboys, this is Memphis Center, go ahead," he replied.

"Memphis Center, One Dallas Cowboys would like to request a right 360," I said. "Lear One Dallas Cowboys, right 360 is approved," came the puzzled reply. We made the 360 degree turn while Jerry laughed and pointed at the contrail he had just bought. I guess Eddy felt compelled to explain ourselves to Center because we knew the inevitable question would arise. WHY?

"Memphis Center, this is Lear One Dallas Cowboys. In case you're wondering, the boss just wanted to see his own contrail," Eddy said. "Are you serious?" the controller replied somewhat bewildered. An obvious Chiefs fan, and no doubt in utter disbelief, he continued his sarcastic onslaught. "Well, you guys are an impressive 2 and 4," he laughed. That was a trivial point in reference to the Cowboys won-loss record. Jerry Jones was always full of himself, win or lose.

What a mark that was, is, and continues to be....

15

"ACE" IN THE HOLE

They were bought for one reason only—speed: Bob Hayes, "Rocket" Ismail, Tim Brown and the Jerry Rices' of the NFL. Sometimes, the gamble paid off. Sometimes, returning kickoffs and being the fastest man in the National Football League just wasn't good enough. Ask Alexander "Ace" Wright.

There was a whirlwind of player signings and contract negotiations from late August until early September in 1990. The season was right around the corner. Jerry finally seemed to buckle down and concentrate his efforts on signing the Cowboys draft picks. Eddy and I flew to Atlanta's Dekalb-Peachtree Airport on August 25, 1990. We picked up "Ace" and his agents and flew them to Dallas. He had missed almost the entire training camp while he waited to sign his rookie contract. It was interesting to watch him try and make it in the NFL.

Still, "Ace" was the fastest man in the league. He was timed at the Cowboys Valley Ranch headquarters at 4.14 in the 40-yard dash. He bench pressed almost 400 pounds. He had all of the physical skills necessary to play professional football. Jerry was a gambler, so he signed him. Gambling on football players and draft picks was a lay-down compared to the volatile arena of oil and gas exploration that Jerry was used to. It was simply another business decision.

During his short-lived playing career in Dallas, he was mainly utilized on special teams, as the Cowboys premier kickoff return specialist. "Ace" did not need a Learjet to fly. He was fast! A small problem soon developed, however. The highly touted, but inexperienced receiver, could not catch the football. It almost seemed that he couldn't even catch a cold. He couldn't learn the system, he couldn't even line up correctly on the ball. I'm sure he was under a lot of pressure to perform in 1990, but we all were. Expectations were high. There were no excuses.

I was sitting in the coaches booth at the Tampa Bay Buccaneers game in Tampa on October 21, 1990, watching the game and listening to Dave Wannstedt, Joe Brodsky, and offensive coordinator David Shula, now head coach of the hapless Cincinnati Bengals. The Cowboys had mounted a fourth quarter rally. They trailed by a mere three points and they were driving. The Cowboys eventually won the contest by a score of 17-13.

"Ace" was lining up. The line judge knew that the wide receivers, from where they were positioned on the field, could not accurately see down the line of scrimmage. The official placed his toe where the line of scrimmage was as a guide. It was a simple way to keep from lining up off-sides. Apparently, catching

Troy's passes was a real problem, he only made matters worse. "Ace" lined up off-sides. The ball was snapped and the penalty flags started flying. It was a stupid rookie mistake and the game was on the line.

They called him "Ace" because he was so fast. One thing was for sure, the only thing he did fast that day was get himself into trouble. Joe Brodsky was one of my favorite coaches. He was the John Madden/Chris Berman of the Cowboys organization. He was more than a coach, he was a real fan of the game. He let his feelings be known regardless. As they lined up to rerun the play, I heard Joe as he leaned back and threw his arms into the air in disbelief. "Ace, you stupid Mother Fucker!" he yelled. The penalty flags flew once again. "Ace" had lined up incorrectly. Twice in a row.

Jerry finally traded him to the L.A. Raiders. He just did not work out in "Big D." With Michael Irvin and the acquisition of Alvin Harper, the Cowboys wide receiver positions were filled. "Ace" became dispensable. Playing for the Raiders, it seems he has finally caught on to catching a few passes. Jerry, of all people, would be the first to admit that "dumb as dirt" is definitely not a permanent state of mind. They thought the same thing about Jerral W. Jones a few years ago when he made his fair share of rookie mistakes.

"Ace" proved them all wrong. So has Jerry.

16

MINNESOTA MIKE

During my travels in Lear One Dallas Cowboys, I learned many things. One, in particular, was it's not such a small world after all. I never dreamed I would cross paths with the son-in-law of the lady in Mississippi that my uncle had the "hots" for. I'm sure the name will sound familiar. His name was Mike Lynn.

It seemed that everything somehow indirectly revolved around the infamous Herschel Walker trade. The same one that the faithful were up in arms about and had called for Jerry's head over. Everyone knew by now that Jerry had, and still has today, the "Midas Touch." He and Jimmy had the ability to make hard decisions on a moment's notice. They knew that the Cowboys needed more than one player, and they needed it fast.

Mike Lynn was then general manager of the Minnesota Vikings. Either Jerry or Jimmy, depending upon which one was asked, orchestrated that blockbuster trade with Minnesota on October 12, 1989.

Afterwards, the Cowboys signed a league leading 16 Plan B veteran free agents. When the team reported to training camp in 1990, my first year as part of the organization, they had 51 players on their roster that had not been to camp with the team in 1989. Rebuilding, with a capitol R, was underway.

After their meetings with Jerry on November 14, 1990, Al and l departed Jet East with Mike and several of his business associates. Also onboard the flight was Victor Kiam, "Mr. Remington," then owner of the New England Patriots. I never knew of his connection with the group. It didn't matter anyway, he has long since been ousted. Jerry loaned Mike the Learjet for a couple of days. It was a simple case of appreciative back-scratching...the least he could do.

They were scheduled for two days of travel with us. At that time, the World League of American Football was being formed. Mike and Tex Schramm were involved and Jerry was glad to help out if it had anything to do with promoting interest in NFL football, i.e. dollars. We departed Dallas that evening and flew to Fayetteville, Arkansas. Mr. Kiam said his good-byes and we headed toward Birmingham.

Several cities all over the world were being awarded their long-awaited pro franchises. We flew them to Alabama for the announcements. The next morning, with the press conferences prearranged, they displayed the teams colors, helmets and logos. There was a lot of media hype and big expectations as they introduced the owner and head coach. The Birmingham Stallions officially became part of the fledgling new World League.

There were cameras, reporters and news media at the Birmingham Municipal Airport as we prepared for departure at Hangar One. We were headed to the second largest city in Mexico—San Antonio, Texas.

During the flight, somewhere between Birmingham and San Antonio, Mike noticed my name placard in the front of the cabin near the door. They were there so that if we did not have a frequent flyer onboard and they had a question or needed something, the passengers could call and ask for us by name. The flight crew preferred to be called by name instead of something like "Hey peon." We slid them in and out as we rotated crews, so the correct names were always visible. Mine read "First Officer Todd Cawthorn."

The flight crew always joked that the real reason was so that Jerry could slide one name out and slide another name in...on a moment's notice. It was the "nothing is permanent" state of mind, that in itself, remains the only thing permanent in Dallas. The same setup is used on the office door of the head coach at Valley Ranch, too. "Cawthorn, now that's an unusual name," Mike said. "Not as unusual as Lois," I replied.

While we were in Birmingham I called and talked with my dad. He told me that my Uncle "Bub" was dating the mother-in-law of the man that operated the Vikings. My uncle lived in Holly Springs, Mississippi, and so did Mike Lynn's mother-in-law. What a coincidence. "You're talking about the second prettiest woman in Holly Springs, next to my wife, of course," he said. "My Uncle "Bub" is dating her," I replied. "You're kidding," Mike said. Neither one of us could believe it. That was amazing.

Mike and I chatted for the remainder of the flight. We were two long-lost pals. The San Antonio Riders were added to the list of World League teams later that afternoon. We departed that evening and flew them back to Dallas/Fort Worth International. Mike and I said good-bye and he boarded his flight north to Minneapolis/St.Paul. The World League lasted about as long as "Bub" and Lois did.

It is amazing how connected we really are and how small the world really is.

17

JERRY'S KIDS

Jerry and Gene Jones have three children. I'm sure no one will be surprised to hear that they were known as "Jerry's Kids." From the outside looking in, I can honestly say that I would not trade places with any of them, not Stephen, the oldest, not Jerry, Jr., the youngest, not even Charlotte, the real love of daddy's life. Always shuttled around from here to there, they were the end result of Jerry's good intentions to keep his family close knit. Isn't it the road to hell that's paved with good intentions?

Stephen, now 31, is the Cowboys Vice-President. He supposedly handled all of the player-agent negotiations for the front office. Make no mistake about it, no one in the front office made any negotiations except Jerry. Period. Stephen graduated from the University of Arkansas, just like daddy. Apparently, he wanted to major in business. Jerry informed him that he would teach him all he ever needed to know about "bidness." What he would major in was chemical engineering. He did.

Charlotte, 28, attended Stanford University, graduating with a degree in biology. She holds a position in marketing for the Cowboys front offices. It was said that it's too bad Charlotte was female because she would have had Stephen's job. Hmmmm.... Brains, beauty, and lots and lots of money. That is an awesome combination. She was off limits to young co-pilots, however. After being turned down one too many times, the pilot that I replaced told me he finally asked her, "Charlotte, what's the matter, you don't like pilots?" To which she replied, "Oh, yeah. I like pilots, my daddy owns three of those." I never asked her out....

Jerral W. Jones, Jr. was the youngest of the bunch. He finally graduated from Georgetown, and is currently in law school at Southern Methodist University. It appeared he was a lot like Jerry. He loved the ladies and he liked a good party. The two of us ended up on the bad side of mama one weekend in Destin, Florida, however. He was late for breakfast one morning 'cause we were being held hostage by two pretty women in my hotel room—all night long. He even had business cards printed that read:

JERRAL W. JONES, JR.
Future Owner of The Dallas Cowboys

I thought they were funny. Before too many of them were passed out, however, Jerry heard about his plan and confiscated all of them. The entire world knows that Jerry Jones, and only Jerry Jones, is the Owner,

President, and General Manager of the Dallas Cowboys. Do not doubt or question that fact. How could Jerry, Jr. have forgotten?

C'mon Jerry, at least let them dream on their own.

18

HORNS, HIDES AND HEADS

Although they lived one state to the north in Springfield, Missouri, that didn't matter. The Joneses never traveled by car anyway. It was only a 35-minute flight from Little Rock in one very expensive and tastefully appointed taxicab, Lear One Dallas Cowboys. For the entire Jones' family, getting anywhere quickly was only a phone call away. A private jet is the only way to fly. Jerry was very close to his parents, J.W. "Pat" and Arminta Jones. Often, when we returned from an away game or an NFL owners meeting, we stopped and visited them.

Jerry's father was a phenomenal success in his own right. First in supermarkets and later in insurance. Jerry learned his merciless business style from him years earlier. Jerry's toy is the Dallas Cowboys. His father's toy is the Buena Vista Exotic Animal Paradise in Strafford, Missouri, located 12 miles east of Springfield. It encompasses 400 acres and is the United States' self-proclaimed "Largest and Greatest" drive-through wild animal park.

There are herds of wild animals and rare birds from all over the world. Approximately 3,000 exotic animals roamed free. There was even a petting zoo for the kids.

The key word was "approximately." The remains of animals that died from sickness or old age ended up as Christmas gifts for the Jones' family. Every kind of animal from Addax to Zebu sometimes ended up roaming free around the airplane's cabin. They obviously spent a small fortune on taxidermy. Bearskin rugs, things with large heads, and every color, shape and size of creatures with horns. Every year I waited and wondered—who had died.

Eddy told me that once upon a time Mrs. Jones scrambled a couple of ostrich eggs for breakfast and probably could have fed 20 people. Thinking back, overloaded the way we always were, an F.A.A. ramp check would have landed us in a pile of trouble. It really was unsafe. If, for any reason we had a fire onboard the airplane, there was no way anyone would have been able to get to an emergency exit. In addition to the "normal" gifts they received, all of those horns, hides and heads were in the way. It would simply have been impossible.

They really were unique gifts. I always pictured Jerry Jr. describing them to his friends along with a "and there I was..." story. We flew quite an assortment of trophies onboard Lear One Dallas Cowboys from Springfield. To Jerry they were just another trophy that he added to his collection. Jerry Jones liked trophies, including the two-legged and four-legged kind. Those were just the beginning. As a matter of fact, he liked trophies so much that he has since started another collection.

A collection of Super Bowl trophies....

19

THE SPIRIT OF ST. LOUIS

Bad things can happen to good pilots with a combination of crew fatigue, bad weather, mechanical problems and distractions. I had been flying Lear One Dallas Cowboys for almost nine months when all of the above conspired to create a nightmare flight.

Eddy and I flew from Dallas through Little Rock and then on to St. Louis, with the entire Jones' family on board. The most important game of the 1990 season was the following day in Atlanta against the Falcons. The Cowboys were in the midst of their dramatic turnaround season, a win against Atlanta would have put them in the playoffs for the first time since 1985.

Rime ice was forming thin and clear as we waited inside the terminal of Million Air at the Spirit Of St. Louis Airport. It was a blue norther day in the dead of a Missouri winter. Moderate icing, turbulence and heavy snow had been reported up to 18,000 feet. It was real co-pilot weather.

An early evening takeoff was delayed because, as usual, they were running late. The weather had deteriorated rapidly. When the Joneses finally arrived for departure, it was late, it was stormy and it was dark. It was worse in Atlanta.

Eddy and I knew that the Atlanta Hartsfield International Airport was diverting due to the weather. We took on additional fuel in case we needed to fly to our alternate airport. As we prepared for departure, we knew in the back of our minds that no one was getting into Atlanta. The plane was de-iced and we taxied down the only runway that was open, Runway 26 Left. It was covered with the "white stuff" faster than the ground crew could clear it.

We completed our checklists and were ready to go. We rolled down the icy runway for takeoff into a blizzard. I pulled the landing gear up. Nothing. I tried to recycle...pull it up, put it down, pull it up, put it down. Nothing. When we taxied down the runway for departure, ice, water and slush had splashed up on the landing gear. It was frozen—in the down position.

The landing gear should only be down at or below certain speeds. Exceeding that speed risked damaging the airplane. On the other hand, keeping the power back reduced the bleed-air. Reducing the bleed-air, or the heat supply to the wings, tail and engines, meant little or no de-icing.

That was not exactly the best situation to be in during a blizzard. Shit, with all of the additional fuel onboard, we could not turn around and land safely in St. Louis. We were much too heavy. There was so much ice and snow on the runway that night, we may or may not have been able to stop. We could not fly all the way to

Atlanta in those conditions with the landing gear down. There was no way the plane would fly with all of that ice.

Meanwhile, they were in the back screaming, "What's going on, what's going on?" Bad weather, mechanical problems and now distractions. Of course, we always, ALWAYS flew tired. Keeping up with the Joneses entailed a ball-breaking schedule.

We were climbing. We needed to get above the icing. Aviating, navigating and communicating. I was watching the radar. Do we jettison fuel and land? Do we keep going? Decisions were being made. Five things were going wrong at once, and they were in the back yelling.

At 20,000 feet the landing gear finally came up and hours later we were in Atlanta. "Atlanta Center, this is Lear One Dallas Cowboys," I said. The Atlanta Hartsfield International Airport was closed....

It was foggy, rainy and bad. Atlanta Approach placed us in a holding pattern. That 20,000 foot climb with the flaps and landing gear down sure burned a lot of the reserved fuel that we had so wisely decided upon in Missouri. How long could we hold? Not for long!

We were paid to make sure that Jerry Jones was always as close to his ultimate destination as possible. We decided to try our filed alternate, the Atlanta-Fulton County Airport. The weather never broke and under much stress and fatigue, and not a sound from the rear, Eddy and I shot a textbook instrument approach. Chuck Yeager would have been proud.

We were the first airplane that made it in almost two hours. Jerry and the family were in the back clapping. They certainly were proud that we made it in there. Eddy and I celebrated with a well deserved high-five as we taxied to the ramp at Hill Aircraft. I slept very well that night.

The Atlanta-Fulton County Airport was near the Six Flags over Georgia Amusement Park. Eddy and I found out the following day that an airplane in the holding pattern behind us held in his pattern too long, became fuel critical, and crashed in a desperate landing attempt.

Unable to make the approach, all six people onboard were killed.

20

WALLY...ER...JERRY WORLD

Flying Lear One Dallas Cowboys was a far cry from riding the infamous station wagon to Wally World. Once we departed Atlanta for the annual New Year's ski trip to Aspen, Jerry Jones and his family came close to Wally World.

Jerry was fit to be tied over the 26-7 loss to Atlanta on December 30, 1990. Former Cowboys "great" Babe Laufenberg, had cost the upstarts a trip to the playoffs. He never played for the Cowboys again. Jerry was looking for a whipping boy to vent his anger and he found "them" in the executive terminal of Central Flying Service, our Little Rock base.

We had planned to stop off and refuel in Little Rock where Shy Anderson, Charlotte's fiance, would meet us with the additional luggage. When he pulled their Suburban onto the ramp and up to Lear One Dallas Cowboys doorway, I knew we had a serious problem. As Eddy and I unloaded skis, boots, poles, leather hats, parkas, Charlotte and Gene's full length furs and jumbo duffel bags, Gene checked each load.

"Be sure the brown leather bag goes on top. That hat needs to go on top. Make sure that my coat goes on top." Finally, Jerry told her, "Godammit, Gene, something has to go on the bottom." Master packers that we were, Eddy and I realized that not in our wildest dreams would we ever be able to transport all of their baggage unless we made two trips. One for the baggage, the other for the Joneses.

Jerry was furious. He just wanted to get to Aspen. This is a man who takes every defeat personally, takes every setback as if he has been hit square in the nose. Jerry's remarkable personal skills were often shelved in favor of his notorious lack of patience. He began to roar, "Get all of this shit inside! I want every single one of you inside—NOW!"

For the next hour he made the entire family unpack and re-pack. Picture this: Here we were in the middle of the executive terminal of Central Flying Service, it was 8:00 p.m. and the entire Jones family was down on their hands and knees, surrounded by mounds of luggage, unpacking and re-packing.

The air was peppered with "Godammit, Gene." The kids were scurrying around trying valiantly to appease Jerry. Cries of "Where is my sweater?" "I just took it out" and "But Mom, I need it" and "Here, I have some room in my bag" rang out.

At first, it was awkward for the flight crew. What could we say? What could we do? Eventually, we joined in the spirit of things and began to urge them on. "You don't need that" and "Here, put that in Charlotte's bag."

Charlotte always packed the best, Jerry, Jr. the worst, and Gene...Gene was impossible.

It was getting late and Eddy and I still had two legs to fly, but the Jones family had to make the critical decision of just what they could live without for a week in Aspen. What a cluster....

21

EL DORADEER

Stephen's fiancee', Karen Hickman, was from the unlikely spot of El Dorado, Arkansas. Located almost 120 miles south of Little Rock, near the Arkansas-Louisiana border, it boasted a population of almost 24,000. She was a sweet girl who had met Stephen while they were both in college at the University of Arkansas. If that scenario sounds familiar, it should. That's how Jerry met Gene. Karen quickly went from El Dorado to "Big D."

The Goodwin Field Airport was a deadly little deer crossing in the middle of nowhere. Seriously! Taxiing down the runway with the lights blazing and the engines revving was standard operating procedure for takeoffs there. That little trick never failed to clear the deer out of our way.

It was a real "white knuckler" to roll down the runway for takeoff in a Learjet at speeds in excess of 150 miles per hour. We just knew a ten-pointer might be standing there, frozen, waiting to nail us. That gave new meaning to the term "road kill." It goes without saying that landing wasn't exactly pure pleasure either.

Eddy and I missed the only approach for landing in my three years of flying Lear One Dallas Cowboys one night at that God-forsaken airport in the southernmost part of the "Natural State." B.F.E. was a politely put understatement. Most of the airports we frequented in Arkansas were like that, however.

El Dorado ranked near the bottom on my co-pilot list of ultimate destinations. To make matters worse, the weather was terrible. Those types of flights always seemed to come up when the weather was awful. It was bumpy and rainy when we departed Dallas that night. We knew the weather in Arkansas was even worse. With no ILS instrument approach, the chances of making it into Goodwin Field were slim to none. We couldn't see our hands in front of us, we flew the approach into a "black hole."

Even in severe weather we may not have had the required visibility to land, but at least we would have seen something—runway lights, an airport beacon, or—something. Of course, by that time it would have been too late to execute a safe landing. In that instance, we would execute a "missed approach," circle around, hold, and try it again.

We never saw anything that night. It was solid blackness. I wouldn't have known if we were at 100 feet or 100,000 feet, had it not been for our flight instruments. Considering the odds that we were up against so many times, only one missed landing is a record I'm proud to hold.

El Doradeer

I've always thought it was unfortunate for us that the runway lights were not working that night we had Stephen and Karen onboard. The Goodwin Field Airport had pilot-controlled lighting. I placed our communications radio on the designated frequency, "clicked" the button the correct number of times, and the lights should have come on. That time they didn't.

Eddy and I missed the VOR approach to Runway 22. Finding the runway was just one of those small little details that a pilot needed to cover. We could not find it in the darkness. With terrible weather and no runway lights, it was not my idea of fun on a Friday night. The only movement on the runway that night were the deer. Why did we even attempt it?

After two tries, we flew to Little Rock. Stephen and Karen had to drive (heaven forbid) back to El Dorado. Stephen was mad. That was the only landing we had ever missed in three years of flying and he was mad. Several virtues and vices seemed to run in the Jones' family. Patience is definitely not one of them.

We didn't care. That was a landing we could live without and quite possibly...we did.

22

MATTRESS THRASHERS

An assortment of the finest suites The Mirage Hotel and Casino in Las Vegas had to offer awaited us. They were all complimentary, of course. Jerry Jones never paid for anything that trivial. A full course steak dinner; blonde, brunette, and red-headed double-breasted mattress thrashers. He also tossed in a long night of high stakes gambling and some Jerry Lee Lewis. The owner of the Dallas Cowboys knew how to throw a bachelor party for his eldest son. It was a nasty job, but God, can I do it again...please?

Eddy and I departed early in the afternoon on February 2, 1991, with Jerry, Stephen, Jerry, Jr., Jimmy Johnson's youngest son, Chad, Cowboys Vice-President and Jerry's long-time business partner, Mike McCoy and Cowboys Director of Marketing, George Hays, onboard. Oh, and Massey, one of Stephen's best friends, who was a Navy helicopter pilot. It was a very diverse group of close friends and business associates. For the first time it was ALL play and no work. We flew Lear One Dallas Cowboys to heaven, or two days of sin and debauchery, take your pick.

We arrived at Las Vegas McCarran International Airport, taxied into Hughes Aviation Services and shuffled into limousines. Several of Stephen's closest and oldest friends from high school and college had already flown in to Las Vegas. A grand total of 20 partygoers lived in the lap of luxury. Everyone was ready to let the games begin! Cowboy, did they ever.

Jerry had arranged one of the private meeting rooms downstairs to be available for the dinner party and for our private viewing pleasure. Everyone met downstairs around 7:30 p.m. We were "dressed to impress" in suits and ties. Well, not everybody. Along with a fully stocked open bar and one of the best steak dinners I had ever eaten, fun, jokes and good conversation were the order of the evening.

Then came the girls. Everyone knows that Las Vegas is internationally known for its 20-minute girlfriends. Oh, if we could all have bachelor parties with girls from *Hustler*, *Penthouse* and *Cheri* magazine. All gloriously nude on the tables, up close and personal. The girls were all over a wide-smiling Stephen. I must admit, in the spirit of the evening, it was plain to see that this was one night that looked like it was going to get seriously out of hand.

They really were beautiful. Stunning combinations of God-given hard-bodies, gorgeous faces and some exquisite craftsmanship by a few well-skilled surgeons. All of the parts were definitely in all of the right places! It was one thing to enjoy some men's entertainment, but quite another to have strikingly beautiful women straight out of the pages of national magazines sign and autograph pictures for us. Everyone was given a complimentary copy of their latest centerfold.

What a performance. They were the most shapely, drop-dead gorgeous and sensuous women I had ever seen. The best part was that each and every one of the goddesses would be "available" later in the upstairs suites. Guaranteed to provide all the lovin' we could handle and then some. Unbelievable. It was still very early. The night was still very young. I was very ready for dessert!

How about a little Jerry Lee Lewis first? Three or four here, two or three there. We all dashed outside to catch taxicabs. Mike McCoy walked out with Massey, Jerry, Jr., Eddy, myself and a few more of the still-amazed. We spotted a Budget rent-a-car van as it pulled through the covered hotel entrance. McCoy motioned to the van driver and with a few well-placed words and gestures, had his attention. He told him, "I've got a party of eight or so. I'll give you $200 to drive us over to the Jerry Lee Lewis concert." We commandeered the Budget van and climbed aboard. We were on our way to the concert. It was only a four block trip. McCoy paid the man and we jumped out.

Our tables were in the front, three or four nice, large round booths for the wild and crazy bunch. First class all the way. Front and center. I don't know who drank the most but I know we gave Jerry Lee a run for his money. The drinks were flowing like a good flight—nonstop. Massey was sitting beside me. He had warned me earlier at dinner that he was a huge Jerry Lee Lewis fan. I had no idea. He was literally shaking in his shoes and he could not sit still. Jerry Lee appeared drunker than we were, he could barely finish a song. Nobody cared. Massey leaned over and said, "Todd, I can't stand it! Let me out...I gotta move!"

I hopped up out of his way. That boy literally stole the show. The entire auditorium was standing room only, packed with people, and he was running up and down the aisles doing some serious shakin'. He caused such an uproar that the spotlight came down on him and the audience loved it! He was tearin' it up. Jerry Lee came over the microphone and wanted to know who was stealing his show. I think he was glad for the help. Meanwhile, it was getting later...almost time for that dessert.

When the memorable show was over we decided it was time to ease our way toward The Mirage. We were primed and ready for some serious gambling. Massey, Chad and myself walked out and hailed a cab. A quick game of rock, paper and scissors determined who paid. It wasn't me. By this time Massey and I had become friends, both being pilots, I guess. Chad was always a lot of fun, we all sat down to lose some money at the $20 Blackjack tables. Didn't take long.

Jerry had well over $500,000 worth of chips in his pocket. He and McCoy were at the craps table blowing hundreds of thousands of dollars. Some of the finest women in Las Vegas that night were along for the ride. Jerry was a magnet and he pulled them in. Stephen was a big gambler too, everyone was having a passable good time. Eventually, some of the few and the proud began easing their way toward the elevators and up to the pleasure palace. Everyone knew that all of those blonde-headed, double-breasted mattress thrashers were nesting up there. Massey and I decided it was time to do a little bird hunting.

Jerry had succeeded in persuading that entire group of centerfolds to do anything and everything that our little hearts desired that evening. Massey and I walked to the edge of the bed and sat down for a private screening. We threw down a few hundred dollar bills and climbed in bed with the dream girl of our choice.

Boy, did I know how to pick em...uh, them. There were condoms from one end of that sin den to the other. Sensual, beautiful and unbelievably sexy. At an early age my mother had warned me about women like that. She was right! It truly was an unforgettable night. God, that was the best dessert I ever had, and no imagination would do them justice.

Earlier in the evening, Stephen had raised a toast to his soon-to-be bride, Karen. Each and every champagne glass was symbolically broken against the wall after dinner. Stephen staunchly swore that he was not going to do it, but we just kept coming, no pun intended, downstairs from the pleasure palace with smile...after smile...after smile. He finally reached the point where he could stand it no longer. He flew upstairs and climbed into the nest.

On our return flight home the next day everyone was looking through their respective magazines, comparing notes and checking out each personally signed picture. I still could not quite believe we had gotten much more than an autograph. Everyone was telling stories and reliving an unforgettable night. Massey cracked a joke to Stephen. It seemed that young Mr. Jones was never circumcised. Apparently, one of the mattress thrashers had asked him, "What are you going to do with all of that foreskin, make a wallet?" I never laughed so hard in all of my life.

Eddy was always one to keep his distance from the boss and he constantly advised me to do the same. I was still their pilot and we did have to return home the next day. As we flew back to Dallas late that afternoon, I thought about the judgment call that I had made—distance myself or take my chances.

Lord, help me—I can't call up any regrets.

23

THE LUST ON THE LOGO

A typical and often asked question was "What do you do during the off-season?" Yeah, right. If they only knew. Off-season—I never heard of the term. There was no such thing as an off-season when I worked for the Dallas Cowboys. Jerry was a workaholic and Head Coach Jimmy Johnson also suffered from workaholism. The flight crew, put it this way: Only workaholics need apply.

Prior to their ultimate and inevitable return to the Super Bowl the Cowboys season was usually finished before the college bowl games began. There was always next year. We then began the scouting trips with the coaching staff. We flew the coaches to the Senior Bowl in Mobile, Alabama, then to St. Petersburg, Florida, for the All-American Classic. Next, we hit the skies traversing the country, visiting every major university of interest. Of course, we always flew to Indianapolis, Indiana, for the scouting combine.

Jerry Jones and the "New Regime"

All of the best college football players in the country, some 400 or so invitees, converged for four grueling days in Indy to showcase their wares. College careers were over, bowl games were forever a part of alumni history and the combine was their last chance for attention before the April NFL draft. A good showing sometimes produced a "sleeper" the scouts had not noticed. Or, perhaps, someone who had been injured and was now healthy and ready to prove his mettle. Most, if not all, of the NFL owners and their coaching staffs were present in the Hoosier Dome to evaluate and talk to the players. The players were in one huge 'meat' market. They ran sprints, lifted weights and most of all, they hoped.

Al and I departed Dallas around noon on Thursday, February 7, 1991. Hubbard Alexander, Joe Brodsky, Dave Campo, Dave Wannstedt, Mike McCoy and Jimmy Johnson were onboard. We flew to Little Rock and Jerry joined the group. Joe Avezzano, Butch Davis, Steve Hoffman, Tony Wise and Mike Woicik had flown up the previous day via American Airlines. The entire Dallas Cowboys coaching staff would be at the Hyatt Regency for the combine.

We departed Little Rock and flew to Indianapolis where we spent the night. Friday afternoon the 8th, after the workouts, we flew back to Little Rock with Jerry and Mike McCoy onboard. On Saturday afternoon we departed Little Rock and flew to Dallas, we picked up Ron Chapman and his group from Dallas' KVIL 103.7 radio station. We flew them back to Little Rock for Stephen and Karen's wedding. It was a tough decision, but football simply had to wait. Jerry's eldest son was getting married.

After the reception was over it was late, but Eddy and I flew back to Dallas with the newlyweds. They were leaving for Australia early Sunday morning for their honeymoon. We probably would have flown them there, but we all would have had to swim. It was too far. A Qantas Airlines 747 was needed for that flight, thank God. We departed Dallas on Sunday the 10th and flew to Little Rock to pick up the Jones' family entourage. We then headed to Jerry's alma mater in Fayetteville, to watch the University of Arkansas versus the University of Nevada Las Vegas basketball game at Barnhill Arena. Afterwards, we flew back to Little Rock late that afternoon. Next, Al and I headed toward Indianapolis with Jerry and Mike McCoy onboard. Some off-season!

Sunday evening we finally arrived in Indianapolis, I was exhausted. I needed dinner and a cold beer. Even though he and Eddy had conveniently switched places somewhere between the nuptials and the hoops, Al agreed that we needed a break. As we headed toward our rooms we spotted several of the coaches in the hotel lobby. After a quick invitation, Al and I went to dinner with Jimmy Johnson, Joe Brodsky and Dave Campo. Dave ate and left while Joe and Jimmy stayed to chat.

"I haven't seen you guys. Where have you been?" Joe asked. "We've been flying the whole time. We had to take Jerry and McCoy back to Dallas and then bring them back here. We have flown non-stop. Eight flights since we saw you guys on Thursday," I said. "Where in the hell have you been?" Jimmy asked. They were astounded. "Oh, we've been to Stephen's wedding, flown some sponsors and took Jerry to Fayetteville for the Arkansas-U.N.L.V. basketball game. We've got four flights tomorrow. What have you been doing?" Al asked, sarcastically. "Jesus! How do you guys keep that kind of schedule?" one of them asked. Then he laughed, "Well, I guess it's no different for you than it is for us," he said.

I knew that the coaching staff worked well into the night on a regular basis. They ate, slept and breathed Dallas Cowboys football. Twenty-four hours a day, seven days a week, 365 days a year. "Yeah, I guess I don't have to tell you fly boys that the lust wore off the logo a long time ago, do I?" one of them said, disgusted. It really surprised me when he said that and I never forgot it. I'll never tell, but feel free to take a guess....

The flight crew never sat still long enough for the logo to tarnish, even in the off-season.

24

THE STADIUM VISUAL

Most people are not accustomed to being airborne in excess of 20 days each and every month. Many of the passengers onboard Lear One Dallas Cowboys were no exception. Not all of the Cowboys coaches were salty travelers. They were not frequent flyers. The flight crew was actually busier and less "scheduled" in the off-season. With the oil and gas trips, scouting trips with the coaches in preparation for the draft, the scouting combine and the many personal and business trips, it was a full-time job. In Jerry Jones world money never sleeps.

We departed Dallas on Monday morning March 4, 1991. The coaches were "scheduled" for four days of scouting in preparation for the upcoming April draft. Onboard was Head Coach Jimmy Johnson, Dave Wannstedt, Butch Davis, Tony Wise, Dave Campo, Joe Brodsky and Hubbard Alexander. Coach Brodsky made no secret in the past of his dislike for air transportation. Four days airborne in a row was more than enough for Joe.

Jerry Jones and the "New Regime"

Our first stop was The University of Tennessee, in Knoxville, where we spent the night. Next, we flew to N.C. State, in Raleigh Durham. A late afternoon departure and we wound up in South Bend, Indiana, at Notre Dame. The next day we continued on to Michigan State, in Lansing, Michigan. Finally, we flew to Lincoln, Nebraska, for a peek at a couple of Cornhuskers. They looked at and evaluated quite a few fellas.

When inflight visibility is good, certain approaches have names. In San Francisco, it is named the Quiet Bridge Visual. In Washington, D.C., the River Visual. In Dallas, it is not surprisingly called the Stadium Visual. What a fine shot it was to fly directly over Texas Stadium and tilt Lear One Dallas Cowboys on its side. That was a view that few ever get to experience.

As we approached the Dallas/Fort Worth Metroplex, we had a sunny, crisp and clear winter day in Dallas. Eddy announced over the plane's P.A. system, "Hey guys, we're cleared for the Stadium Visual. Do you want us to dip the wings a little bit so you guys can look down on your office?" he asked.

Coach Brodsky, always close to the emergency exit, muttered something under his breath but of course the rest of the coaches were excited to see it. As we flew directly over Texas Stadium we turned the Lear a full 90 degrees on its side. We were virtually "hanging" into the hole. It was one hell of a view. Everyone was yelling with all the excitement of a winning field goal in overtime. Well, not everyone.

Brodsky was sitting in the seat directly behind my co-pilot's seat. The man shit. He yelped and screamed until we finally touched down on terra firma. "You S.O.B.'s are trying to throw me out of here, goddammit, I can't believe you bastards," he screamed. All of the coaches died laughing at Big Joe. He was a picture perfect "white knuckler."

He thought we would simply dip the wings a little bit and he would look down. He had no idea, and if the truth was known, the other coaches were probably a little surprised themselves. He didn't know we were going vertical, straight over Texas Stadium's trademark. As pilots, day in and day out, we had to devise our own forms of entertainment.

It was all in a day's work.

25

JERRY'S FRIEND

He knew it; she knew it; we knew it; they knew it. Everyone knew it. No one ever talked about it, however. Everywhere from Bourbon Street in New Orleans, Louisiana, to his private box at Oaklawn, the horse track in Hot Springs, Arkansas, in Dallas, and Destin, Florida, and at the duck club in Stuttgart, Arkansas. From Little Rock to Las Vegas. The girlfriend went.

What a girl. Tall and voluptuous with olive skin, dark eyes and stylish short brown hair. She was one long legged, full breasted, amazon looker. A fresh 31 years of age. Her most important attribute, however, was convenience. Susan Skaggs worked for Texas Stadium Corporation.

Does Gene know? Who knew? Every place Jerry Jones went, she went, just not at the same time. It had been too close to call more than once. We hustled the "friend" and her luggage out one door at Jet East, moments before Gene surprised everyone and walked in another.

Jerry Jones and the "New Regime"

Everyone at Jet East knew what a "girlfriend trip" was. When those flights came up, and they came up much more often than anyone ever imagined, Jet East knew we had to park the car and get the "friend" and her luggage into the airplane as soon as possible. If the Dallas Cowboys could run a "two-minute drill" that efficiently, they would never lose a game. Probably a little more than a touchdown at stake there, however.

The funny thing about Jerry, it was almost as if he challenged anyone to tell. He would frequent places where he knew he would be instantly recognized. He had a popularity in Little Rock, rivaled only by that other now infamous Arkansas native, Bill Clinton. In his hometown, where everyone knew his wife, he took his "friend" out in public to all of the local dance clubs and bars.

We flew Jerry and his "friend" into Hot Springs to watch the horse races in a private suite he and Gene owned. Down in the French Quarter people instantly recognized Jerry Jones. He would sit on the patio at the Inn on Bourbon Street, smoozing, hugging, drinking and lovin' all over his beautiful young "friend." He was so careful to hide that particular trophy from Gene's eyes.

If Gene was in Dallas Jerry would arrange a "jump and run." In other words, an unplanned "business" trip to Little Rock. Upon arrival, he would actually get in his Mercedes and spend the night in his Little Rock mansion on Pleasant Valley Drive with the girlfriend. Make that his and Gene's mansion. He made no secret of it as long as it was out of Gene's immediate vision.

Of all the places he took his "friend," and with the many people that he saw, it was blatantly obvious to

Jerry's Friend

even the most casual observer! This had been going on for years and years! Most assuredly, during the several years I was there, they were heavily involved. They spent more than a lot of time together. I hear they still do....

One Friday evening Jerry and his "friend" arrived at Jet East. They were all lovey-dovey in the back of Lear One Dallas Cowboys, laughing and drinking. Obviously, they were looking forward to their weekend rendezvous. Before we had even taxied to our departure runway, they were in the back hot 'n' heavy. Jerry and Susan were mixing more pleasure than business. A Lear 35A is not exceptionally large. We could feel the airplane moving and shaking. It didn't move and shake that long; talk about a two-minute offense. I looked over at Al and Al looked at me. Al raised his eyebrows and grinned. We laughed.

Jerry Jones lives for two things. He loves women and winning. So far, so good. I was grateful for his attitude one time, however. At Jet East there was a real nice pilots' lounge. With a big screen television, two separate bunk rooms with beds and a shower. It helped ease the pain of endless waiting, sometimes.

We had been at the airport since early morning, and as usual...still no passengers. I dialed for love. I called one of the girls that I had been seeing. She said she would come "wait" with me. We decided to order some Chinese food and kick back in the pilots' lounge, so to speak.

I was away from home quite often and it had been awhile since we had seen each other. Into the bunk room I went with a "friend" of my own. I guess Eddy must have told Jerry, "Todd has some girl here." They searched all around Jet East for several minutes. Eddy finally paged when they couldn't find me. Jerry

93

was standing there in the lobby and burst out laughing when I came tearing out of the bunk room zipping up my pants.

As Jerry and I walked out to the airplane for departure I was apologetic. "Jerry, I'm sorry, I didn't know you were here," I said. "Todd, that's alright, you know I never condemn anyone for getting laid!" he replied.

He winked. Then he laughed.

26

THE PRIDE OF PORT ARTHUR

Beaumont/Port Arthur, Texas, was proud to claim Jimmy Johnson as a hometown boy. He was named Coach of the Year by the Associated Press after the 1990 season. The city threw a big banquet and brouhaha for him on May 17, 1991. Eddy and I flew Jerry and Jimmy to the Jefferson County Airport for the evening's festivities at the Beaumont Civic Center. It started out festive, it ended up fiery.

Similar to pre-departure drinks on a commercial airliner, Lear One Dallas Cowboys could become the site of many a gathering of friends. Sometimes, just the curious would stop by to visit before takeoff. Too, Jerry liked to show off his Learjet to the ladies. He gave them a tour of his impressive white chariot. They sat on the couch, mixed several drinks and listened to the CD player.

Jerry played his favorite tune and self-described theme song first. *"Mama's don't let your babies grow up to be Cowboys,"* by Willie Nelson, echoed loudly into the humid night. It became a rich man's tailgate party. The mixing and mingling had finally ended and the two J.J.s and their very special guest, former Cowboys "great" Lee Roy Jordan, flew back to Dallas around 10:30 p.m.

Eddy and I didn't need a hearing aid to catch on that a heated discussion was taking place in the rear of the airplane. When we landed, Eddy hit the ground running. "Todd, you take care of everything, I'm gonna try and catch the red-eye to Little Rock," he said. Eddy grabbed his personal taxi service, one of the line service fellas from Jet East, for a free ride to Dallas/Fort Worth International.

The war of words was still going on so I stood outside the door for awhile. Everyone was off the airplane except Jerry and Jimmy. They were pouring drinks and palavering until I started to worry about the airplane's batteries. They cost almost $4,000 each and I sure did not want to be responsible for $8,000 worth of juice. I thought they would deplane any minute, so I waited.

Almost 20 minutes later I stuck my head in, "Excuse me Jerry, if you are going to be awhile, I need to have them hook up a ground power unit so we don't run down the batteries," I said. "Yeah Todd, go ahead and do that," Jerry mumbled. I called line service over with a G.P.U. and they plugged it in. If only the problem inside the airplane could have been solved that easily. Not a chance....

I was still standing by Lear One Dallas Cowboys door when I started feeling uncomfortable. The discussion had escalated very rapidly. Jerry was known for his self-indulgent God complex and when he was drinking...well, we know his record. Jimmy was red-faced and animated. The pressures had mounted and a shouting match was taking place in the Lear.

Jet East has large sliding glass doors, so I walked into the terminal and decided to watch the fireworks from inside. Occasionally, I could here them yelling all the way inside the terminal. I could see them through the windows. They just sat in the airplane drinking and yelling. The rift between the egos was slowly but surely headed in a public direction.

The crux of the problem on that night was the NFL draft held a few weeks earlier. Jimmy was a master planner when it came to the draft. No staff worked harder, or prepared more thoroughly than Jimmy and Co. He felt very strongly they could have handled the draft alone. He knew which pieces would fit the Super Bowl puzzle. He was still very upset over Jerry's antics in the "war room" on draft day. I stepped outside to hear Jimmy scream "It's not a dog and pony show!" Ouch....

Jerry still seethed over the snub and he didn't give a damn if Jimmy was "Coach of the Year" or not. He had to have the last word then, and always. Ironically, the Cowboys '91 draft was a coup. Russell Maryland, Alvin Harper, Dixon Edwards, Godfrey Myles, Erik Williams, Curvin Richards, Tony Hill, Darrick Brownlow, Leon Lett and Larry Brown made the active roster. I'm sure they would never believe the trouble they caused.

That was supposed to have been Jimmy's night in his hometown. It went from 11:30 to 12:00 then 1:00 then 2:00. Finally, at almost 3:00 a.m. I knocked on the door. "Jerry, line service can take care of everything, do you mind if I go on home?" I asked. "No Todd, go ahead, go on home," he said. I had just witnessed the beginning of the end. Again.

That was that. Jerry and Jimmy sat in the back of the airplane for at least five hours I know of when I counted the flight time. Not so privately they vented their hostilities. I thought they were friends. That exchange was all business. To this day, I don't know what time they finally went home. Jerry always had something to say and Jimmy had gotten real tired of listening. The world would soon know that there was no love lost between the two of them. That May evening was certainly no exception.

I don't think anyone would have ever dreamed that Jerry and Jimmy's ultimate demise would have happened so quickly and at such an unfortunate time. It was not that abrupt. As I looked back, I realized that I had seen it simmer from the very beginning. Their feelings ran deep, strong and personal.

Jerry Jones picked a strange place to end his friendship with Jimmy Johnson in 1994. The back of Lear One Dallas Cowboys that night in 1991, however, was a pricey and private place to start. As Jerry's ego continues to evolve, the front door at Valley ranch will continue to revolve.

Mark my words....

27

MAMA WAS MAD

She was a former Arkansas beauty pageant winner. Jerry and "The Mrs." were slowly but surely becoming accepted in Dallas, and things were looking up. She had also accomplished something that Jerry never will. Unlike her husband, she made the city's "Ten Best Dressed" list. She could afford to look good— and she did. There was only one thing she was on that day, however.

Eugenia "Gene" Chambers Jones was mad. Mad at the "other" men in her family. Gene knew how to let her true feelings show without saying one word. She made sure there was no mistaking them. She was sitting directly behind me facing toward the rear. That was definitely not her normal seat in Lear One Dallas Cowboys. Gene did not want to be anywhere near those "hoodlums." Mama was mad. Real mad.

Jerry and Stephen had taken Jerry, Jr. out on the town in Little Rock the night before and they had stayed out late. They finally came home, very late, and very,

very drunk. Jerry, Jr. was her baby boy and when he was out with "those two," she knew they were up to no good. To top it all off, he had been sick the week before with a terrible cold. What Jerry, Jr. needed was rest, not a long night of heavy drinking and bar-hopping with dad.

The rest of the family was sitting in the back cutting up, teasing each other, telling jokes and laughing. They were just having a good time. Normally, when a group of people are laughing, you can't help but laugh with them. But not Gene. She was not speaking to anyone. That was definitely not the first time Jerry found himself accidentally on purpose in Gene's dog house.

I did not actually hear the punchline of the joke that Stephen was telling, but I recognized the sound of Jerry, Jr.'s voice as he started laughing. He laughed so hard that it made me laugh; then I heard him sneeze. He was unable to cover his mouth in time, and out shot a huge loogey. The green monster went airborne, flew across the seat, and nailed Sr. right on his lapel. Uh oh.

It must have stunned him and everyone else for a split-second. I heard him as he snarled, "goddammit Jerry." It was too late, the damage had been done. I turned around and saw him delicately wiping his jacket with a paper napkin. There was an eerie silence as everyone cringed and awaited his reaction. He grinned, burst out laughing, and the entire family joined in, almost on cue. If the airplane had been big enough they would have been rolling on the floor.

When Gene realized what had happened, well.... She was mad at Jerry to begin with, he had gotten exactly what he deserved. "I told you he was sick," she said, laughing.

Jerry didn't mind. For once, it was only a big loogey that flew his way. It was only a loogey.

28

HOT SAUCE ANYONE?

Whether he was dealing with a recalcitrant player who had just begun his long and arduous hold-out from the sweatbox of Cowboys training camp, or the livid wife who waited for him at the airport, Jerry Jones did not play defense. One sentence or one second was all it took and Jerry was on the offensive. He was an offensive guard, remember? Late one evening while we waited with Gene at Jet East, Eddy and I received a lesson on how to play offense from a master of the game.

For whatever reason, and we just never knew with him, Jerry had finally arrived. He was very, very late, and very, very drunk. He had stopped on his way to the airport and picked up a bag of tacos. He was basically a "happy" drunk with taco sauce dribbling down his chin.

Gene was very upset as Jerry happily settled onto the couch in the rear of the airplane. Gene, who definitely knew how to push Jerry's hot buttons, began her attack. One sentence into her diatribe and Jerry cut loose; it was venomous. "I am sick and fucking tired of you always putting pressure on me. Don't I have enough goddamn pressure in my life?" he screamed. Thinking to myself that this particular flight was taking us to a nice relaxing weekend in Destin, Florida, things seemed a little out of hand.

Nevertheless, Eddy and I completed the before taxi checklists and turned Lear One Dallas Cowboys onto the parallel taxiway for Runway 13 Right at Dallas Love Field. The verbal play by play grew louder and louder. "I do everything for everybody! I take care of your mother, I take care of your brother, I take care of your sister!" he was still screaming.

After a lengthy litany of the names of every cling-on from hell he could think of, he fell back on the old standby, "If I want to have one little drink I will." Suddenly, and while we were still taxiing, Jerry yelled to the cockpit. "Stop this fucking airplane right now, we're not going anywhere!" he screamed. We stopped the airplane.

At that point, Gene realized she had a razorback by the tail. She calmly said, "Look Jerry, let's not ruin the trip, let's not ruin our weekend, please let's go on." The razorback squealed, "This is my plane and if I don't want to go, we don't go—anywhere!"

Here we were, stopped on the taxiway. Eddy and I were caught in the cross-fire, afraid to turn around and look in the back. Fortunately, no other aircraft were behind us. I didn't know if or when it would all end. The offense sputtered to an occasional "I bust my ass" and "This is my plane...my fucking plane."

Jerry Jones remained as unpredictable as Texas weather. Another sudden and violent outburst definitely deserved attention and sent Gene running for cover. The ferocity and relentless nature of his attacks were sometimes downright frightening. It seemed that he had embraced the philosophy of his new mentor, long-time NFL "loose cannon" and Raiders owner, Al Davis. Davis's "I'd rather be feared than respected" philosophy, seemed deeply rooted in Jerry's psyche, also.

Gene shrugged off the spectacle as if it were a common occurrence. He was a man possessed and on the edge. He simply needed to unwind and relax in the Florida sun. Thirty minutes later, we were well on our way. I decided to sneak a peek to the back. There was Jerry Jones, the proud owner of "America's Team." He was passed out, drunk, and asleep. He still had hot sauce on his chin.

We were in Destin within the hour, it rained all weekend....

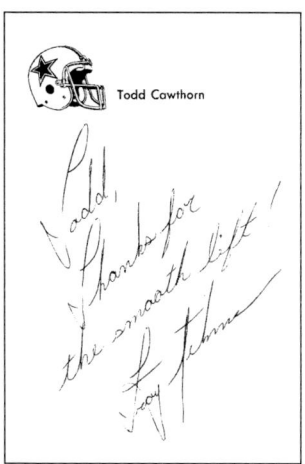

One of the nicest fellas ever onboard Lear One Dallas Cowboys, and most certainly Dallas' favorite son. A cowboy mamas could hope their babies grow up to be. Quarterback Troy Aikman.

A true Dallas Cowboys legend. He was the former anchor of the Cowboys "Doomsday Defense" in the 1970's and is now a prominent businessman. It was a genuine thrill to meet the great Lee Roy Jordan. Lee Roy was the first Cowboy inducted into the Ring of Honor under the "New Regime".

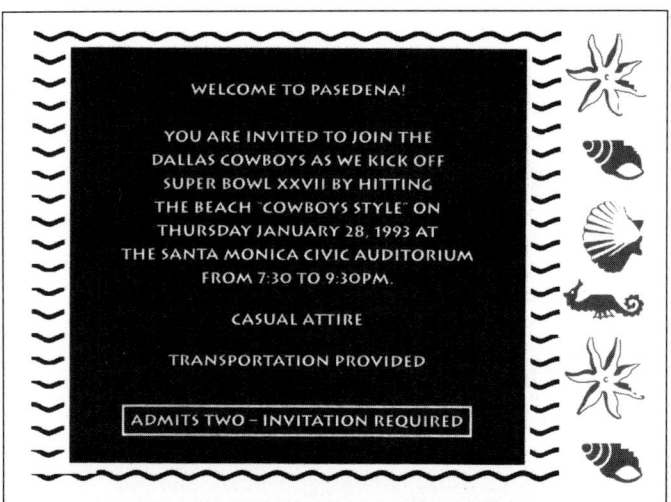

It was an exciting time for everyone as the Cowboys returned to their first Super Bowl since 1977. The Cowboys hosted an informal kick off party on Thursday prior to Super Bowl XXVII against the Buffalo Bills.

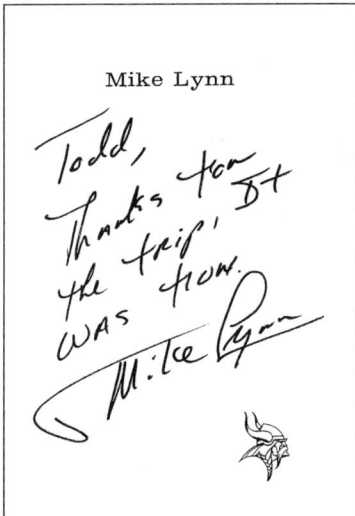

Former General Manager of the Minnesota Vikings, Mike Lynn, and Cowboys Owner, Jerry Jones, Orchestrated the blockbuster 'Herschel Walker Trade' in 1989. Mike was a pleasure to fly and quite a generous man. He deserves at least partial credit for rebuilding the Cowboys.

Bash was an understatement. After the Cowboys complete trouncing of the Bills 52-17, words cannot describe the amount of electricity, or the amount of alcohol, in the Santa Monica Civic Auditorium that night. Jacket, tie and invitation required. Jerry was vindicated. Jimmy had conquered. Life was good.

My official pass ensured complete access, cafeteria food and 100 degree temperatures during Cowboys training camp at St. Edwards University. An average of 100,000 fans take advantage of the rare opportunity to see their favorites each summer - free of charge.

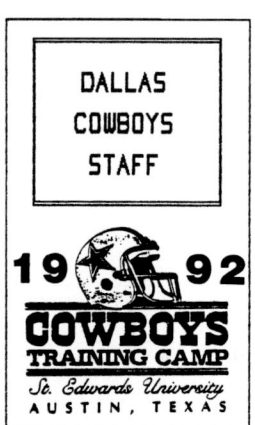

The controversial and outspoken former Viking, Cowboy, Falcon and current Miami Dolphin linebacker Jesse Solomon. Jesse and Jerry feuded like the Hatfields and McCoys.

AMERICAN AIRLINES 727-200 CHARTER SEATING DIAGRAM		( ) INDICATES RETURN ONLY					NEW YORK LAVATORY	
COATS & STORAGE				ROWS	GALLEY & FOOD SERVICE			
A		B			D	E		F
JOHNSON, Coach Jimmy		WANNSTEDT, Dave		3	JONES, Stephen		DIXON, Jack	
TURNER, Norv		WISE, Tony		4	DAVIS (McCOY, Mike)		AVEZZANO (McCOY, Joni)	
ALEXANDER, Hubbard		BRODSKY, Joe		5	ANDERSON, C. (Jones, Jr.)		ANDERSON, Shy	
A		B	C		D	E		F
(Avezzano, Joe)			WOICIK, Mike	6	CAMPO, Dave		SLOWIK, Bob	
FORD, Robert			(Davis, Butch)	7	ARMSTRONG, Neill		HOFFMAN, Steve	
PELLETIER, Dave			Lacewell (Dalrymple)	8	GLIEBER, Craig	(McCoy, Jeff)	JOHNSON, Chad	
Arnold - KKDA	Vasquez - KVIL		Hansen - KVIL	9	Sham, B. - KVIL	Sham, P. - KVIL	Thomas - KVIL	
Sommer - KLIF	Wallace - KVIL		Simpson - KVIL	10	Williams - WBAP	Park - KDFW	Swanbeck - KDFW	
Lindstrom - KTXQ	Herrera - KXAS		Rhadigan - KXAS	11	Aguilar - KXEB	Montez - KXEB	Quintero - KXEB	
Miller - KRLD	Gant - WFAA		Riba - WFAA	12	(Weber, John)	HIRSCHFELD, T.	Bayless, Skip	
REY, Michael	GREENE, Roger		PURCEL, Scott	13	MORRIS, Chris	Rodriguez - KTVT	Menefee - KTVT	
MURRAY, Jack	SERPA, Derek		UNTERBERG, Dr.	14	SCRIBNER, Ron	SPAIN, Ron	BROWDER, Jim	
HOLMES, Clayton			WOODSON, Darren	15	WILLIAMS, Erik		GANT, Kenneth	
VEINGRAD, Alan			GOGAN, Kevin	16 EX	GESEK, John		HELLESTRAE, D.	
SMITH, Vinson			NEWTON, Nate	17	TOLBERT, Tony		ABRAMS, Bobby	
CORNISH, Frank			TUINEI, Mark	18 EX	NOONAN, Danny		CASILLAS, Tony	
SMITH, Emmitt			ROBERTS, Alfredo	19	HARPER, Alvin		BROWN, Larry	
MARTIN, Kelvin			IRVIN, Michael	20	MYLES, Godfrey		EDWARDS, Dixon	
HOLT, Issiac			HALEY, Charles	21	NORTON, Ken		WASHINGTON, J.	
WRIGHT, Alexander			JONES, Jimmie	22	JONES, Robert		SMITH, Kevin	
ELLIOTT, Lin			SAXON, Mike	23	AGEE, Tommie		WILLIAMS, Robert	
RICHARDS, Curvin			LETT, Leon	24	BATES, Bill		HORTON, Ray	
HENNINGS, Chad			NOVACEK, Jay	25	BEUERLEIN, Steve		AIKMAN, Troy	
MARYLAND, Russ			JEFFCOAT, Jim	26	STEPNOSKI, Mark		JOHNSTON, Daryl	
MAURER, Jim	TOUCHET, Scott		VANDERMEER, Dr.	27	O'NEILL, Kevin		COCHREN, Don	
	GALLEY			28	McCORD, Mike	CARICHOFF, Steve		
	GALLEY			29	(Mays, Bruce)	BLACKWELL, Rbt.		
				30	BUCHANAN, Buck	ZAMORANO, Dr.		
	LAVATORY					LAVATORY		

Although we spent countless hours waiting at airports for Jerry Jones, it was time to call the roll when the Cowboys charter departed. Coaches, media, staff and players each had assigned seats.

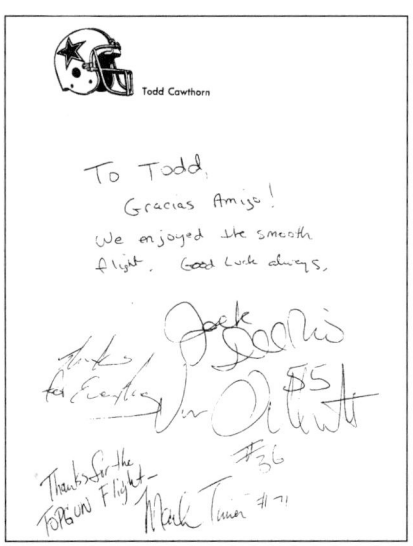

A fantastic three day trip to Ixtapa, Mexico. Starting middle linebacker for the Vikings, Jack Del Rio, Cowboys All-Pro tackle, Mark Tuinei, and former Cowboys safety, Vince Albritton, enjoyed a well-deserved vacation with their better-halves. Lots of fun.

Good 'ol Lear One Dallas Cowboys. I spent many days and nights in the cockpit of Jerry Jones well-traveled, and now internationally known, 1979 Learjet 35A. I became a 500 mph fly on the wall.

Prior to departure for Canton, Ohio, and the induction ceremonies for legendary coach, Tom Landry, into the Pro Football Hall of Fame in 1990, distinguished members of the "Old Guard" posed with Eddy and I for posterity. From L-R: Me, Dick Nolan, Robert Newhouse, Drew Pearson, Ed "Too Tall" Jones, Jethro Pugh and Chief Pilot Eddy Collins.

At the intersection of Cowboys Parkway and Valley Ranch Parkway, two blocks east of MacArthur Boulevard in Irving, is the Dallas Cowboys posh Valley Ranch headquarters and training facility.

In the unlikely event the huge star located on the corner of the club's headquarters didn't catch your attention, don't despair. A wall to the left of the main entrance will alert you to your destination. A proud reminder of the Cowboys four world championships. Two and counting for the "New Regime."

ITINERARY
DALLAS COWBOYS VS. NEW YORK GIANTS
Meadowlands Hilton
Two Harmon Plaza
Secaucus, New Jersey 07094

Saturday, September 29, 1990
12:00 p.m.	American Airlines Charter departs for Newark, New Jersey
4:21 p.m. (EDT)	Arrive **Newark International Airport**
4:35 p.m.	Depart Airport for Hotel
5:00 p.m.	Arrive and Check in the **Meadowlands Hilton**
5:30 p.m.	Team Meeting/Walk-Through T.B.A.
7:00 p.m.	Dinner in the **Rivercove Room**
8:30 p.m.	Special Teams Meeting in the **Riverside 1 & 3 Room**
9:00 p.m.	Meetings:
	Offense in the **Riverside 10 Room**
	Defense in the **Riverside 1 & 3 Room**
10:00 p.m.	Snack in the **Rivercove Room**
11:00 p.m.	Bed Check

Sunday, September 30, 1990
8:00 a.m.	Wake-Up
8:30 a.m.	Pre-Game Meal in **Ballroom A & B Room**
****	* * * * Taping Begins * * * *
9:00 a.m.	Meetings -
	Offense in the **Riverside 10 Room**
	Defense in the **Riverside 1 & 3 Room**
9:15 a.m.	Chapel in the **Riverside 10 Room**
9:45 a.m.	Early bus departs for Stadium
10:30 a.m.	Team Buses Depart Hotel for **Giants Stadium**
****	<u>**Check Out of Hotel - Pay Personnel Charges.**</u>
	REMINDER: It is your responsibility to pay incidental charges, i.e., phone, movies, etc. If you do not pay at check-out time, you may be fined up to 5 times the amount.
11:00 a.m.	(Media and Guests Depart Hotel for Stadium)
11:00 a.m.	Team Buses Arrive **Giants Stadium**
11:55 a.m.	QB's, Kickers, Snappers, Kick Returners on Field
12:05 p.m.	Receivers and DB's on the Field
12:15 p.m.	Remainder of Squad on the Field
12:40 p.m.	Clear Field
1:00 p.m.	**KICKOFF VS. NEW YORK GIANTS**
4:30 p.m. (ETD)	Buses return to Airport following the Game
6:00 p.m. (ETD)	American Airlines Charter departs for Dallas
8:36 p.m. (ETA)(CST)	Arrive **DFW Airport**

Monday, October 1, 1990
****	(A.M.) - Weight Lifting as scheduled with Coach Woicik
10:00 a.m.	Sick Call: ALL injuries and/or illness report to the Training Room for Treatment and Rehab
****	ALL Players must check into **Training Room** by 1:00 P.M.
2:00 p.m.	Team Meeting
4:15 p.m.	Practice (Treatment and Rehab to follow)

Tuesday, October 2, 1990
10:00 a.m.	Treatment and Rehab in the **Training Room**
	* * * * D A Y O F F * * * * *

The Cowboys were always required to be in the host city at least 24 hours prior to kick off. A detailed itinerary for each away game helped keep everyone in order.

Once a fan, always a fan, and still of the Dallas Cowboys biggest fans. This picture of Santa and me was taken Christmas 1972. I was six years old.

My favorite captain, Al Devens. I occasionally had to remind him that the war was over, but he was a good pilot and a good friend.

St. Edwards University is located approximately three miles south of downtown Austin, the Capital of the State of Texas. It is the only state capital that is the training camp home of an NFL franchise.

Training camp is usually held from mid-July to mid-August. Some of the activities each year include the Cowboys Golf Tournament, the Blue-White Game, scrimmages with other NFL teams and autograph opportunities.

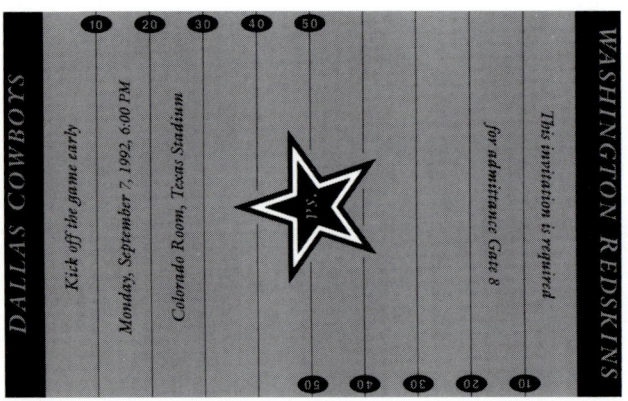

Jerry and Gene Jones truly lived and enjoyed the "jet set" lifestyle. They often entertained friends, VIPs, and celebrities from all across the country prior to kickoff at Cowboys home games. The red carpet treatment required an invitation, however.

29

THE 50 MILLION DOLLAR MAN

It's great to know that Cowboys quarterback Troy Aikman really is a Cowboy that mamas could hope their babies grow up to be. Jerry thought highly of him, also. He must have, who else was capable or able to squeeze 50 million out of Jerry Jones?

Troy was definitely Dallas' favorite son and the only player Jerry ever gave Lear One Dallas Cowboys to for anything other than a business related flight. A college friend of Troy's from U.C.L.A. was getting married. Eddy and I departed Dallas on Thursday afternoon June 6, 1991, and we headed west.

Troy and close friends Tom and Missy Whitenight and long-time buddy Doug Kline, were onboard for the three hour flight to The John Wayne/Orange County Airport in Santa Ana, California.

Everyone knows that June is the month for weddings. Unfortunately, Jerry had forgotten that his only daughter, Charlotte, would be getting married on the same Saturday and she needed the Learjet. Jerry provided first class seats on American Airlines for their transportation home to Dallas. The normally quiet, reserved and unassuming quarterback and his friends were having a great time.

They sat in the back and listened to country music all the way. Lear One Dallas Cowboys ten disc compact disc player received a real workout. George Strait, Willie Nelson, Jerry Lee Lewis, K.T. Oslin, George Jones and Randy Travis provided personal concerts all the way to California.

They played cards and drank beer. Since Doug worked for the local Bud Light distributor, they drank several beers. Unlike some of the "other" Cowboys players, however, Troy traveled at a high rate of speed, with two designated drivers.

That was one of the nicest trips I ever flew. Troy was thankful for the smooth lift and he told us so. Money had not changed Troy Aikman. He still stayed in touch with old friends and he kept his head on straight.

He was first class all the way—to the Super Bowl.

30

THE LOTTERY

Shy had somehow done it. He had closed the deal of a lifetime. A commoner and employee of AllTel, a cellular communications company in Little Rock, had achieved the impossible. David Shy Anderson married Charlotte Leigh Jones on June 8, 1991, at Pulaski Heights United Methodist Church. He had won his own personal version of the lottery: Jerry Jones only daughter.

Eddy and I flew black ties and their ladies to Little Rock with the help of two Learjets, One Dallas Cowboys and another chartered from Jet East. Eddy and I flew "1DC" while Al and a "loaner" pilot flew the other. It was more like an event than a wedding - to the tune of $80,000 for the dress, $100,000 for the fresh flowers and a vintage Rolls Royce convertible for the ride from the reception to the airport. Jerry did well by his daughter on her wedding day.

It was, however, the most beautiful event I had ever seen. Charlotte looked stunning—how could she not?

Shy just stood there grinning. The reception was an elaborate black tie affair at The Little Rock Country Club. That spectacle alone had to cost a small fortune. At least it helped to explain the sharp increase in ticket prices for the Cowboys home games the following season. After the reception the captains switched, Al and I flew the newlyweds to Dallas for the night.

Charlotte was excited the following morning when the Anderson's arrived by limousine at Jet East. Shy had chosen a surprise destination for their honeymoon. Only Al and I, Shy and Jerry knew of their ultimate destination. We knew because we had to file flight plans. Shy knew because it was his idea. Jerry knew because it was his money—uh, airplane. I wondered which one Jerry would miss the most, his daughter or his Lear.

It was almost a six hour flight to their destination. First we would fly to Fort Lauderdale, Florida, and refuel. Then across the Bermuda Triangle, south to St. Maarten in the Caribbean Islands. Shy and Charlotte would then board a small boat that would shuttle them across the bay. Her surprise honeymoon destination was Anguilla.

Shy had always taken a keen interest in flying. He had even entertained the thought of becoming a pilot by taking some lessons in Little Rock. In the past, he would come up and sit between us in the cockpit so he could ask questions, listen to the radios, and enjoy being a wanna-be. I knew it wouldn't take him long before he realized that the seats in the back of Lear One Dallas Cowboys sat much better. I was right.

After we departed Fort Lauderdale, there was nothing but beautiful blue ocean below us. We were

The Lottery

well into the flight when Shy finally made his way to the cockpit. After the usual quizzes, questions and small talk, Al and I began to ask Mr. Jones, uh— Anderson, a few questions of our own. Al had been married for hundreds of years so there was not much he would add to the conversation. I, on the other hand....

"So, Shy, Charlotte still doesn't know where you're taking her?" I asked. "Nope, I won't tell her," he replied. "I bet she has ways of getting it out of you if she wanted to," I teased. "Yeah, you're right about that," he replied, laughing. "You know we're more than halfway there, what can you tell me about Anguilla?" I asked.

Al and I knew, unfortunately, we weren't going to stay. We would drop the love birds off, get them on their way, then it would be six more hours of flight time home. Plus, we had to clear U.S. Customs in Florida. It may have been their honeymoon but it was not blissful for the flight crew. All that meant to us was a minimum of 12 hours worth of flying in one day. I knew that Jerry would miss his Lear the most. He let his daughter go, but "1DC" had to come back...soon.

"Well, we'll be staying at Jumbay Bay, a very exclusive resort," Shy began. "The resort is all private villas and a 20 minute boat ride will take us across the bay to it. She is going to be real surprised. The one bedrooms start at $1,200 a night," he said. "But, since it's the off-season, I'm getting the suite for about $600 a night," he continued. I knew they would not be staying at anything less than a grand honeymoon suite. Made sense to me. People typically went to the islands in the winter. "Must be nice," Al said. "Yes sir, this place is very exclusive and very private. It is reserved for the very, very rich," he proudly said.

Shy had been married for less than 24 hours and he proved my theory as we spoke. He looked me in the eye and said, "Guess what? I am now very, very rich." Then he laughed, went to the back and sat down with his very, very rich new wife.

He quickly found the seat—with his name on it.

31

THE DEVIL IN MR. JONES

Before Al's wife, Judy, became ill, the flight crew worked an ideal schedule. It was the only way to operate under the circumstances and schedule that we kept. For a short period of time, Eddy, Al and I actually had a semblance of a "normal" life. We worked two weeks on duty, then one week off. I flew one week with Eddy, one week with Al and then I was off for a week. That was great. I was able to work hard then play hard. Once Judy became sick, however, Al began to feel the pressure and I believe he began to feel guilty.

Judy was placed on a three week schedule for her chemotherapy and it just wasn't working well with our two week duty schedule. Al felt that he needed to spend more time with her. Everyone understood that. The right thing to do would have been to hire another pilot in the interim. Jerry Jones has trouble knowing the right thing to do sometimes. Even if he knew the right thing, occasionally it had to be forced upon him.

Jerry Jones and the "New Regime"

In the summer of 1991, Eddy and Al were in Destin, Florida, with Jerry and Gene. I was in Dallas and my beeper was turned OFF. To this day, everytime I hear a beeper, I recoil in fear. They were supposed to fly home to Dallas, then Eddy and Al could go home to Little Rock. Apparently, when Jerry arrived at the airport, he said they were going to stop in Dallas and then go to San Francisco for the next several days.

Al said that he really needed to go home. Jerry overheard him as they loaded the luggage prior to departure. Jerry made a comment and it really hurt Al's feelings. He had been flying Jerry for five years at the time, he didn't have to put up with it. He had retired from the Air Force as a full-bird Colonel. With his military pension and investments, he was financially secure. Al flew because he loved to fly.

Although Al never repeated to me what Jerry said, I gathered it was not something that should have been said to anyone, much less a man that had flown Jerry and his ego through the gates of hell and back. Due to his military background and based on the many war stories that he had told me, I knew that Al had seen, heard and been through much worse. Al was needed at home. Judy was terminally ill with cancer.

For Al to have been that upset, it had to have been vicious and severe. I know of no one in the entire Cowboys organization that was ever removed, or immune, from Jerry's insensitive wrath. His demeanor often changed in an instant.

After Jerry and Gene were onboard, Al told Eddy, "When we land in Dallas, I'm getting off. You can find someone else to fly it. I'm not going to San Francisco, I'm going home." Eddy ran inside and called me from

The Devil In Mr. Jones

the terminal before they left. I had just walked in from the pool. "Todd, I think Al's gonna quit. Get your bags together, we're going to San Francisco. Meet me at Jet East in two hours," he said, adamantly. Shit!

Jerry was in the back, fuming. The flight crew was in the front, disgusted. They could hear the conversation in the back. Gene told Jerry, "You get up there and apologize to Al, you proud son of a bitch." Jerry wouldn't. "You're going to lose one of the best pilots you have ever had. You get up there and you apologize," she said. He refused.

Finally, less than 20 minutes outside of Dallas, Al said that Jerry walked up and apologized. He was sorry he said what he did and he didn't want Al to leave. If he was thinking about quitting, he wished he'd reconsider. About six months later Al asked for a permanent leave of absence, Jerry never hired a replacement pilot.

Eddy and I managed the impossible. The two of us flew Jerry Jones rigorous schedule by ourselves. We were on permanent reserve 24 hours a day, seven days per week, for well over a year. That was no way to live and eventually I could not handle it. I stayed until the bitter end, but I was becoming burned out at 26 years of age.

I had been willing to sign a three year contract. I still worked for peanuts. I wasn't quite as eager as I had once been. I experienced a somewhat startling revelation of an unwritten requirement if one intended to play even a small part in Jerry's "New Regime."

Just like all the others before me, I sold my soul to the devil. The Devil in Mr. Jones.

32

NEVER SAY...NEVER

Jerry Jones ran wide open on the ground as well as in the air. Few things ever seemed to slow him down. Keeping up with Jerry didn't leave a man time to breathe, I learned to eat and sleep whenever I had the opportunity. It was all I could do to keep up with the man at an average speed of over 550 miles per hour. So, to everyone else I say: good luck.

One Indian Summer day early in June of 1991, opportunity knocked on a Cadillac window in a no parking zone in front of the Texas state capitol in Austin. Whether it was for training camp, some big business back-scratching, or maybe some political lobbying, Lear One Dallas Cowboys spent a lot of time flying into and out of Austin. That particular trip we flew Jerry and one of his attorneys to the capitol.

As we deplaned at Page AvJet, Jerry had a strange request for me. "Todd, I don't know how long I'm gonna be at the capitol. I don't want to stay there and be visible for very long. You come along and drive around the block until you see me then I want you to pick me up. In the meantime, you get to ride in the back...see how it feels," he said. Right. See how it feels. I would have felt more comfortable in a level six thunderstorm.

I knew that the day before on his way to the airport, Jerry came sliding up to a stop sign and was stopped by a Dallas policeman. He was going 65 miles per hour in a 35 mile per hour zone. He was on the telephone. He had no driver's license, no insurance and no proof of registration. I've often wondered how many of us would have gotten away with all of the above. It's obvious how that turned out. That back seat ride to the state capitol building turned out okay, too. I'm still here.

Jerry and his attorney jumped out running and headed into his meeting. I climbed into the driver's seat, and as I was pulling out, a group of construction workers motioned me over. "Is that Jerry Jones, the owner of the Cowboys?" they asked. "In the flesh," I replied. "What's he doing down here?" More questions. "I don't have any idea. He just wants me to drive around and pick him up in a little while," I said.

I was hoping in the back of my mind that I would be able to find a place to park and still keep an eye out for him. "Oh no, that's not necessary, you can park right here," one of them said. If I had only known what lay ahead, I would have refused the offer and driven the wheels off that car.

There were signs everywhere: No parking, No parking, No parking. There were construction barricades everywhere, too. Didn't matter, they wanted to talk. Talk Dallas Cowboys football. We should run the wishbone and line Nate Newton up as a tailback. Yeah, sure we should. Don't you guys need to go whistle at girls, pull your pants up, maybe get back to work, or do...something, I thought. After almost an hour of non-stop conversation, I was exhausted.

That meeting lasted forever and that Cadillac seat became too soft. When Jerry finally came out, what was Todd doing? "Wake up Todd," Jerry was laughing. "You remind me of my kids. If I told them to wait on me, they would be doing the same thing," he said. I was supposed to be driving around, but I was piled up in the front seat, sound asleep. I had bad dreams, however. Nate Newton had just scored his first NFL touchdown. Troy Aikman was the lead blocker, and as usual, Jerry Jones was on the sidelines. He wasn't standing there to be seen, smooze or enrage. I looked twice, he had a headset on. It could happen.

Never say never, stranger things have happened in Dallas. Wait and see....

33

WE FLY FOR FREE

The old adage for a corporate pilot is "We fly for free and we get paid for waiting." A truer statement has never been spoken. Especially, when we were trying to keep up with the Joneses. That was exemplified on virtually every flight as well as during training camp in 1991. Eddy and I had been flying the "1DC shuttle," in and out, back and forth, between Austin and Dallas all month long.

It was a very demanding and rigorous schedule during the uncertainties of Dallas Cowboys training camp. Executives, radio personalities, news media, corporate sponsors and players. We flew them all. After another long and busy day, we were settled in for the night at the Austin Hilton, or so we thought.

On that particular August night Jerry's daughter, Charlotte, one of the Cowboys marketing and special events coordinators, had planned the annual festivities at Hooter's Restaurant for the media. It was scheduled to be over around 10:00 p.m., that was about the time Charlotte called.

"Eddy, I need to take off at 11:00 p.m. for Little Rock. We will be dropping mother off in Dallas," she said. The kids could say they needed to use the airplane and with Gene onboard, Eddy did not question the order. We dashed up, threw our bags together, climbed into our uniforms and raced to the Robert Mueller Municipal Airport. That procedure was affectionately known as a "jump and run."

It was late at night so Page AvJet, our Austin home away from home, kept only a skeleton crew. They worked with one man on the counter and one man on line service. Eddy and I began the drill to calculate and place a fuel order, check the weather, file a flight plan and have the airplane brought up. "Sir, this is going to take awhile. You are parked in the very back of the hangar with six planes in front of you," he said. Great, I thought.

We handed over the credit cards and patiently waited while line service methodically moved one plane, moved another plane, then another and moved still another. Phew. Finally, our lone line serviceman had Lear One Dallas Cowboys brought up, front and center. Quickly, now how about some fuel? Done. All pre-flight interior, exterior and cockpit checklists were completed. An exterior walk-around; everything looked good. By then it was 11:15 p.m. and we were ready for departure.

No Charlotte. No Gene. No big deal. We were well used to waiting. Media night was over so no one was available for us to contact. I stretched out and buried deep in one of the overstuffed La-Z-Boy recliners in the pilots' lounge. We thought it was rather strange when 1:00 a.m. passed, then 2:00. Not nearly as strange as 4:00, then 5:00. At 7:00 a.m., people had begun walking into the terminal, probably for something I had never experienced, an on-time departure.

Eddy and I were still sitting there, the definition of grunge. We had been awake since 8:00 a.m. the day before. We looked exactly like what we were, two corporate pilots, half asleep and half awake, as we waited and waited and waited. Our passengers might arrive any minute....

At—you guessed it, 11:00 a.m., Charlotte and Gene waltzed into the terminal. I bet they were glad they didn't have to "waltz across Texas" with us. Eddy and I had put in a 30-hour duty day. We still had to fly! Why? Because they didn't tell us and we didn't ask: Is that night or day? We flew on "supposed to's and rumors."

We fly for free...we get paid for waiting.

34

HOPPIN' MAD

Locking keys in the car with the motor running is not an easy thing to own up to, but is there a family out there who has not done it? Late one sweltering Dallas afternoon we flew into Jet East with Gene and Jerry onboard, they were running late as usual. Gene desperately needed to head in one direction and Jerry was late for the studio taping of his television show, "Cowboys Special Edition with Jerry Jones." It was an inside look at the team, formerly televised on CBS affiliate KDFW Channel 4 in Dallas.

Within a few miles of the airport, we were close to arrival. I radioed Jet East, "Jet East, this is Lear One Dallas Cowboys, we're about ten minutes out, we'll need Jerry and Gene's cars." One of the nicer services provided at Jet East was for a select "few", their cars were waiting, air conditioned and ready to whisk them away almost before the airplane's engines were shut down. Of course the airplane was based at Jet East so everyone was well aware of what had to be done.

Jerry Jones and the "New Regime"

Jet East was extremely busy on that particular day but when Lear One Dallas Cowboys and Jerry Jones called it was "two-minute offense" time. We quickly taxied to the ramp, Gene retrieved her luggage, hopped into her jet black convertible Jaguar and disappeared. Jerry raced into the executive entrance of Jet East's main terminal and into the crew rest lounge with suit in hand.

Having been told the urgency of Jerry's plight, one of the always helpful line service personnel loaded Jerry's luggage into the back seat of his new dark blue Cadillac and accidentally locked the keys in his car. It was on the tarmac with the motor running! Jerry ran out straightening his tie and reached for the door. The unthinkable had happened. He started hopping around like a deranged toad. Late for the studio, sweating like a toad, embarrassed in front of all the other airplanes that had begun to stack up, Jerry went ballistic. Jet East brought up one of their courtesy vans in record time and rushed him to Channel 4.

Two days later, Eddy and I were waiting at Jet East for yet another adventure, when I heard the line service fella was gone. Permanently. He had done absolutely nothing wrong! He was simply trying to help. It certainly did not matter what the circumstances were that surrounded the humiliation, or the fact that a human mistake was made. He was just another innocent victim.

When Jerry Jones was hoppin' mad—everyone quickly cleared a path.

35

HOW 'BOUT THEM CHEERLEADERS!

Since 1972, they have lined up on the 20 yard lines of Texas Stadium, every quarter from the first to the fourth. They rotated, so regardless of seating, the fans always had a "new" group of 12 to gaze upon during all of the Cowboys home games. They are, remember, the world famous Dallas Cowboys Cheerleaders.

Jerry Jones had almost come full-circle in the public relations department since his foot-to-mouth comments in 1989. For that accomplishment he can thank the firm of Fairchild-LeMaster and Rich Dalrymple, the Cowboys Director of Public Relations. Together they softened some of Jerry's rough edges. Lear One Dallas Cowboys had proven to be a high speed PR vehicle in itself. That logo on the tail would only go so far, however.

The cheerleader pictures that we carried onboard were much more popular than the team's pictures—by a wide margin. We gained additional service from the many aviation companies that we flew into in exchange for complimentary pictures of the 48 Dallas Cowboys Cheerleaders.

The names of the ladies were listed on the back of each full color 8x10 photograph. Anyone could match the beautiful face with the name of their favorite. As we handed them out, the standard one-liner was "the pictures were free, but the home phone numbers would cost extra."

Supposedly in effect was a long-standing "rule" concerning the inevitable desire to fraternize between Cowboys employees, players, etc., with the cheerleaders. Rules were always meant to be broken, but the new Cowboys organization provided a different twist. It simply depended on who broke them. Troy Aikman always did as he pleased more than once, as did Jerry, Jr..

Owner in training, Jerral W. Jones, Jr., walked directly in his daddy's footsteps when it came to apprehending beautiful young women. The cheerleaders proved that there were no "rules." He began "fraternizing" with one of them so I asked him if she would be going to Florida with him over the weekend. "She hasn't quite made it to that status yet. She's not private jet material," he replied bluntly. Hmmmm. A beautiful, blonde, Dallas Cowboys cheerleader was not blue-blooded Arkansas royalty and Gene had not given her stamp of approval.

After my first flight to Cleveland on September 1, 1991, I felt sorry for the flight crew of the Browns. How was a man supposed to get extra perks working for an organization with no cheerleaders? The Cleveland Browns are the only franchise in the National Football League without cheerleaders. Too bad.

How 'Bout Them Cheerleaders!

We arrived at Cleveland Stadium, the oldest in the NFL, for the opening game of the Cowboys 1991 season. We were beating the Browns fairly handily and with an airshow in progress at Burke Lakefront Airport next door to the stadium, the faithful seemed more interested in the F-16s flying overhead than they were with the Cowboys 26-14 victory.

Except for the "Dog Pound." Loud and boisterous, with intermission music guaranteed to keep their fans excited, those famous end zone dwellers were hoopin' it up. They lived in Cleveland, they sat in an outdated stadium, their team's colors were brown and orange and to top it all off, they don't have any cheerleaders. But, they do love their Browns.

I was in the press box with the sportswriters who came to the games with computers and laptops. Breakfast and lunch was provided for all the sports media and team representatives in attendance from across the country. Prior to the game and at halftime, everybody lined up just like at a cafeteria.

I was standing in line when I struck up a conversation with one of the Browns' PR assistants. Who cared about the Cowboys or the Browns? I had a few important questions and I needed some answers. "Where are the cheerleaders? I don't see any," I said. "Cheerleaders, we don't need any. We have the Dog Pound," he replied. I knew that sometimes we took our talented Texas beauties for granted, but he couldn't fool me. I knew the real reason the Browns didn't have any cheerleaders.

Maybe it's because they just don't have 40 pretty girls in Cleveland.

36

R-E-S-P-E-C-T

Some of the airports that we flew into were extremely small. The boy may have left the country but the country never left the boy. After 6:00 p.m. there was no line service, no flight service and no tower available. That in itself created some additional problems for the flight crew, but as usual, we always handled it. As long as Jerry Jones was not inconvenienced we had jobs. A perfect example was Destin, Florida.

We were "supposed to" fly to Little Rock but Little Miss Susan Kneepads (as she was known throughout the organization) decided that she would rather go to the beach instead. Since Jerry was in like Flinn for a long weekend at his beachfront home with his 31 year old mistress, the plans had changed. They went wherever she wanted to go. Always.

In the summer it is one of the most beautiful beaches in the world. Unfortunately, it is located in the panhandle of northern Florida. Destin's weather in the winter was definitely not babes in bikinis. It was cold. Cold like deep south cold, with temperatures in the upper 20s. That pleasant sea breeze became just plain windy. It was not summer, it was cold.

Except for the "locals", Destin seemed to close down in the winter. We were "supposed to" return to Dallas around 3:00 p.m. Sunday afternoon. No problem. Al and I requested a late checkout from the Holiday Inn and around 2:00 p.m. we headed to the airport. As usual, one hour before "scheduled" departure.

There was not much activity at Miracle Strip Aviation that cold winter day so we asked line service to pull the airplane up front. They parked and fueled it. Al and I returned our rental car, completed our departure checks and sat around the terminal talking with everyone who worked at the airport.

Our "scheduled" 3:00 p.m. departure soon passed. It quickly became 6:00 p.m. Remember, this was the only airport in Destin. This was the only terminal in Destin. After 6:00 p.m. on Sunday (especially during that time of the year) they shut the place down. They literally seemed to roll up the streets. The airport employees left, Al and I had no choice but to leave with them. They locked up the facility...now what? Talk about being left out in the cold.

Nowhere to go, nowhere to stay. We should have been used to it by then. If they were not planning on going home shouldn't they tell their pilots? We had flown into and out of Destin at least a thousand times. Jerry knew that the airport closed at 6:00 p.m. It was "first the nose, then the toes" cold. I sat outside the front of the terminal and stared at the airport entrance. Where were they? Finally, I'd had enough.

R-E-S-P-E-C-T

I am not an official member of the "Piss and Moan about Everything Club" but this was ridiculous. I was accustomed to waiting all day long but having to wait outside at night in the cold, that was it! In desperation I walked over to the lot where all of the rental cars were parked. I pulled on door handles praying that one was unlocked. The entire time I thought to myself, "No wonder they went through four pilots in two and a half years before I came along." God, it was cold.

Oh, for the days when a coat hanger could open a car door. It was a miserable, blistering cold. I had no doubt it was very, very warm where Jerry was. Nestled up between those.... I'm sure he did not forget. I'm sure he could have cared less. He had other things on his, uh, mind.

Meanwhile, the two people that enabled them to be there in the first place were at the airport freezing to death. It was pitch dark and I was praying for a careless car attendant. Finally, I found it, the lone rental car in the entire parking lot that was not locked. There was a God.

Jerry and Susan finally arrived at the airport around 9:00 p.m. Where were the pilots? We were huddled together in a rental car and damn glad to be there. The moral of the story: It doesn't matter how wealthy you are, it only takes about ten seconds to pick up the telephone, call and tell someone if you were going to be late.

We knew the reason. We didn't know the reason. Who cared the reason! It was just common courtesy. That type of insensitivity happened so often in that "glamorous" job, that finally I resigned myself to one fact.

Jerry Jones has absolutely no common courtesy or respect...for anyone. Period.

37

SAVE THE CHILDREN

It was a good thing we had a $1,000,000 per year flight department budget. We must have spent a minimum of $3,000 annually just trying to get our passengers to show up, much less on time. Here's how we worked it. We ordered a pizza or had some Chinese food delivered. Or even better, we would send one of the fellas from line service to Wendy's for one of Dave's burgers.

It never failed. "Low and Behold" the passengers would show. That little trick endeared me to line service forever. They always ate my food and I always departed hungry. Eddy and I outsmarted ourselves one time up in Calgary, however, and we almost starved to death.

Jerry, Stephen and Karen, Mike McCoy and his new wife Joni, had gone to Canada for an oil and gas meeting on Friday. Oil and gas was always on Jerry Jones business agenda. Several times per year we flew north of the border. Calgary was home to one of Jerry's many oil and gas companies, The Arkoma Production Company of Canada.

The Cowboys had a game in The Pontiac Silverdome against the Detroit Lions on the following Sunday, October 27, 1991. Takeoff was "scheduled" for Saturday morning. As usual, Eddy and I were at the Calgary International Airport bright and early. Good thing we had eaten a quick breakfast because it would be our last meal for a long time to come.

We had a "supposed to" departure time around 11:00 a.m. I resigned myself to the fact that it would be just another late lunch. Afraid to leave the airport and go somewhere for lunch, Eddy and I just hung around the executive terminal of Field Aviation. When Jerry and the group finally arrived around 9:00 p.m., a mere ten hours late, we were rump sprung and ravenous.

I knew we faced a three hour flight and a razoo through United States Customs. I began to salivate when I smelled the food they brought with them onboard. They had gone to dinner earlier that evening and brought along some leftovers.

A lot of things happen when one crosses international lines. Each and every passenger has to complete citizenship documentation, show their passport and fill out several forms. Occasionally, the flight crew has to take all of the luggage off the airplane for inspection. Clearing customs is a time-consuming minor inconvenience. It had already been a very long day for Eddy and I, and it was far from over.

There was a hierarchy for the seating in Lear One Dallas Cowboys. Jerry sat in the far left rear on the couch, always near the phone and compact disc player. The "bigger" or more important they were, or thought they were, the farther to the rear in the club seating area they sat. The seating then graduated toward the front where the real peons sat. That was us, the ones flying Lear One Dallas Cowboys.

Mike McCoy's beautiful wife, Joni, was sitting near the front of the airplane directly behind my co-pilot's seat. Joni was a flight attendant. She met Mike while working on one of the American Airlines charters. She had been a flight attendant long enough to know. Out of kindness, she leaned forward and asked us if we were hungry. We were. She fixed us a small plate.

Jerry realized what she had done and told her, "NO!" He refused to let her give us any of their "leftover" food. Just as she was preparing to hand it to us, he flatly refused. We continued to the Oakland/Pontiac Airport, cleared customs and taxied to Aerodynamics, Inc.

Sunday afternoon I was waiting in the hotel lobby to depart for the Silverdome. I spotted Joni as she walked up. Before I could even say "Good afternoon" she said, "Todd, I am so sorry. I felt so bad for you guys." What else could she say?

We just never knew which Jerry Jones was going to show up on any given day for any given flight. Maybe the meetings had not gone to his liking. Maybe someone had said something that peeved him. Maybe he was giving Karen, Stephen's new wife, lessons on how to handle the hired help.

No maybe...about the flight crew being hungry.

38

DAMN YANKEES

Ten minutes flight time from Little Rock was Jerry's infamous "Duck Club" in Stuttgart, Arkansas. The Joneses made a habit of being there often around Thanksgiving and Christmas. The whole family was involved. Sometimes, even Charlotte and Karen hunted ducks. It was, in my opinion, the mosquito capital of the world. Many people besides Jerry Jones frequented Stuttgart for some of the finest duck and geese hunting to be found anywhere.

Carl Humphrey operated the Stuttgart Municipal Airport. He fancied himself to be a Chicago O'Hare International control tower operator. He called it The Stuttgart International. Every time we landed, which was often, he always had homemade biscuits for the flight crew. The shuttle van was always there to take Jerry, the family and their friends the 15 miles or so to Jerry's private "Duck Club." Carl was a great guy and he could tell a good story, too.

One night during the hunting season, several years ago, Carl had already gone home. Perry, the airport security guard and night watchman was the only one left. He was working the gate. When a plane landed the passengers had to get through a security gate for access to the airport entrance. Once through the gate, they could drive the few minutes to the surrounding hunting areas. There were dozens of private "duck clubs" in the area, Jerry's was one of many.

A Lear 55, which is a slightly larger version of the Lear 35 that we flew, arrived at almost 2:00 a.m. The passengers assumed that the gate was locked at that time of the morning and that there was no one there to help them through. They were attempting to drive around it. Perry heard all of the commotion and hastily went over to check things out. "What are you doing?" he asked. "We need to get through the gate, can you open the gate for us?" came the reply. The person he was talking to did not fit the image of a wealthy "duck club" owner, or even an invited guest for that matter.

"I'm Ted Nugent," he said. "Yeah, right. If you're Ted Nugent, then I'm Elvis fucking Presley. I need to see your drivers license," Perry replied sarcastically. It really was Ted Nugent, the "Motor City Madman." Ted and Tommy Shaw, formerly of the band Styx, had formed a new band together. It was called Damn Yankees. They had flown into Stuttgart as the invited guests of another wealthy Arkansan.

With a name like Damn Yankees, Ted and Tommy quickly realized that they didn't qualify for very much southern hospitality.

39

THE SILVER AND BLUE SLEIGH

Jerry and Gene Jones believed in Santa Claus, so he naturally paid them a visit. Look up in the sky this Christmas and there might be a giant Lear-sized contrail following Santa's sleigh because Lear One Dallas Cowboys will be bringing up the rear.

Springfield, Missouri, was one freezing cold, miserable place to be on any 23rd of December. Regardless of where they were, the Joneses flew there every year to be with Jerry's parents. One day and one night in Springfield and then Christmas Eve afternoon we flew to Little Rock.

Eddy and Al lived in Little Rock so they were home for Christmas. We always arrived with just enough time for me to catch the last Southwest Airlines flight home to Dallas. It might as well have been just another hotel key in Little Rock, however. I often spent Christmas day by myself. All of my family was in Georgia and most of my friends had long gone home for the holidays. I don't mind saying it was lonesome. In those days, Christmas dinner with a friend at Chili's was a good day.

We were never supposed to fly on Christmas day, but every year they called. Southwest Airlines did not have flights available Christmas day and I could not get from Dallas to Little Rock on another carrier—it would be too late. One would think that for just one day out of the year...just one. Eddy and Al had to leave their families to fly the Joneses to El Dorado, Arkansas, to spend some time with Karen's parents. Lear One Dallas Cowboys pilots took away from their own and made sure the Joneses were where they wanted to be, when they wanted to be there. Like I said, it was a full-time job. The Joneses had Christmas, no doubt about that.

We made several trips back and forth from Dallas to Little Rock with Gene. We helped Santa get a head start, box after box after box and package after package after package. The line service personnel at Jet East that were entrusted to help us load the silver and blue sleigh, muttered to themselves, "I ain't believin' this!" Believe it.

When it came time to fly toward Springfield, we somehow managed to get the Joneses, and their gifts, in the Lear. With all of the gifts packed around them, I swear all I could see were the whites of their eyes. Now, where did you say that emergency exit was?

Once we arrived in Springfield, we unloaded all of the gifts for his parents. The following day we loaded all the presents and packages his parents had given them to take back to Little Rock. I literally had to climb over packages just to get to the door. Our helpful line service elves had to help move boxes out of the way just to get the Joneses out; then, we crawled back in to get the rest of their packages. It was purely amazing.

The Silver And Blue Sleigh

It was close to Christmas one year and, as usual, we were waiting at Jet East when Gene called. "Todd, this is Gene. I'm having a watch delivered to the airport, all you have to do is sign for it. Oh, and make sure Jerry doesn't know about it, see you later," she said.

I waited. I signed the paper receipt. I was holding Jerry Jones $20,000, solid gold, Piaget watch. I slipped the box in my jacket pocket and I began to worry. Big square links of gold for the band. I had just signed the receipt for a watch that may or may not have been the right one. A solid gold watch...$20,000. Jerry's watch was in my pocket!

When we arrived in Springfield, Eddy and I began the timely process of unloading the sleigh. Jerry motioned me over to the side of the airplane. "Todd, I've got Gene's ring in my bag, I really don't want to leave it on the plane overnight. Do you think you could hold it for me 'til we get to Little Rock?" Jerry asked. He was so casual about it and it caught me off-guard. "Sure, be glad to," I said. "Thanks, see ya later," he replied.

It made sense that he would not want to leave it on the airplane overnight because we rarely ever locked the sleigh, uh, Lear. Jerry did not want to take a chance in case someone went Christmas shopping in the airplane. I did not know that the damn thing was a custom made $60,000 ring! The receipt was in the bag and like a damned fool I had looked at it. I slipped it in my pocket and then I really began to worry.

Gene didn't want Jerry to know. Jerry didn't want Gene to know. I knew. I knew I had $80,000 worth of Santa Claus in the left and right pockets of my flight jacket.

If memory serves, I slept in my flight jacket that night.

141

40

STAYING ALIVE, STAYING ALIVE

What he did was deadly; we shouldn't have been there in the first place; we had no business in the high heavens flying a Learjet into the Merrill C. Meigs Airport in Chicago, Illinois, late on the afternoon of December 28, 1991. A Lear 35A is capable, depending upon conditions, to make it into and out of small airports. I preferred at least 5,000 feet of usable runway. Any pilot will say that for takeoff and landing, any runway length left behind was of no use. Just wasted space. Meigs Field, with 3947 feet of runway made me feel like a test pilot.

I still don't know the reason. Whether for convenience (Meigs is just across Lakeshore Drive from Soldier Field), lack of common sense, fear of the job or whatever. Eddy had set us up for another one of those wild nightmare flights. It was the 1991 N.F.C. playoff game and the Cowboys first post-season trip since 1985. It was against Mike Ditka and "Da" Bears.

Meigs Field is primarily a VFR airport, VFR meaning: Visual Flight Rules. In other words, it helped to see where we were going to land. It is only 21 nautical miles away from Chicago's Midway Airport, a commercial airport, where we should have landed in the first place. I guess a 25-minute limousine ride for Jerry Jones was just too far.

The weather was bad, not so much thunderstorms and lightning, but overcast with slight drizzle and a very low lying cloud layer. Midway Tower recommended, and we accepted, an ILS approach down to about 900 feet. We would break off the instrument approach once we descended below the cloud layer at Midway and fly "visually" to Meigs Field. That was the plan, or so we thought.

One would have thought that with several airports in such close proximity to each other that the controllers at Midway would have called the tower at Meigs to relay some useful information. For example, "We have a Learjet that will be breaking off the approach at 900 feet on the ILS, on a heading of zero-three-zero degrees...coming your way." This could not have been, and was not the first time, some poor misguided soul wanted to park a Learjet at Meigs Field in marginal weather.

Here we were, flying the approach, no problem. As reported on the ILS to Runway 31C, we broke out of the cloud layer at 900 feet. We had ground contact and Midway in sight so we made a right turn, cancelled our IFR flight plan and headed in the direction of Meigs Field. No problem. All Jerry and the Joneses knew was that with the flaps and gear down, we appeared to be landing. That reported 900 foot cloud layer was not exactly accurate. We were flying into and out of the clouds as we headed to Meigs. Some of the buildings in Chicago don't just seem tall, they are tall—REAL TALL! We could not see where in the hell we were going. Suddenly, we had a very big problem.

The conditions of our plan were that when we broke off from the approach at Midway, we were on our own with no air traffic control until we contacted Meigs Tower. We were supposed to proceed visually. It should not have been a problem, and under normal conditions, it wasn't. However, Meigs Field is located on the shores of Lake Michigan. Rain, low lying clouds and the moisture in the area had produced a rolling fog. Very similar to that of San Francisco. It was very unpredictable.

Under marginal weather conditions, according to Federal Aviation Administration regulations, proceed to your destination under special VFR and remain clear of the clouds for obvious reasons. Pilots can't see very well in the clouds. We were not even on a flight plan anymore...just ducking and diving...flying through the clouds headed toward Meigs. Frantically, I called Meigs Tower. "Meigs Tower, Lear One Dallas Cowboys is with you, 900 feet, inbound for landing," I said. He had no idea we were coming!

"Learjet inbound, say your position, maintain VFR and remain clear of Meigs airspace! I've got a King Air taking off!" he replied a little agitated. I bet he was not nearly as agitated as that King Air pilot. I can imagine he was thinking the same thing I was. He was in an airplane blasting off into "the soup" when out of nowhere there was suddenly a Learjet in the pattern. Neither of us knew where the other one was! Holy...I was about to shit. Eddy was in a panic. We had no A.T.I.S. which is the aviation abbreviation for Automatic Terminal

Information System. Handy little service. It gives pilots a real secure feeling to know which runway was currently being used, what approach was in use, the current temperature, winds and other pertinent airport information. We had none of the above.

Since Meigs Field was only 21 miles from Midway Airport, we entered the traffic pattern based on the reported winds at Midway. We entered going the wrong way. Meigs Tower was spittin' bullets! In marginal weather, air traffic control had an outbound turboprop King Air flying one way, an incoming Learjet flying the other, and...well. Thank God we had the presence of mind to descend. We did. We were over Lake Michigan.

Meigs Tower was pissed! We made a 180 degree turn near midfield, came in and landed on the correct runway. Jerry was in the back yelling, "What in the hell is going on?" All they knew was that we appeared to be landing, then we headed another direction, we made a 180 degree turn back in the other direction, we were real low over the lake, and finally we landed. Salty travelers they were, but this was not exactly the smoothest flight we had ever made. Old Jerry was the least of our problems.

As we taxied toward the ramp of Butler Aviation, Inc., our friendly ground controller politely gave us the phone number to the tower. He also said that we may want to give them a call—immediately. "Eddy, I don't think it would be a good idea for you to call them," I said. "Why not?" he asked. "I think you had better go see them personally, oh, and don't forget your kneepads. You know what you're gonna have to do," I joked. Eddy knew I was right. It just didn't pay to think of the world of shit we had not so smoothly flown ourselves into.

The Federal Aviation Administration could have been called. Not Good. What did Eddy finally decide to do? What any desperate man would do. The only thing he could do. He grabbed a handful of Dallas Cowboys Cheerleader pictures! Those pictures were usually reserved for line service personnel, customer service representatives and for "as needed" public relations at the numerous airports that we flew into. It was an emergency and we definitely needed their help. Dallas Cowboys team and cheerleader pictures always seemed to garner a night or two of free hangar space, unlimited use of courtesy cars for the crew and other "perks." Eddy decided to let the beauties do most of the talking for him.

The tower controller, after a fairly lengthy discussion—maybe the pictures weren't enough after all—finally agreed that the problem was not so much our fault, as it was a problem of coordination between the airports in close proximity to the busiest airport in the world, Chicago's O'Hare International. Luckily, he still had a place for pictures of beautiful women.

After the Cowboys 17-13 win over the Bears the following day, I was in the cockpit performing the pre-flight checklists. I was computing our performance figures for departure—how much fuel we could take on, how many feet of runway we would use for takeoff and what our aircraft weight would be, based on fuel load and number of passengers.

One of Butler Aviation's line service fellas walked up and leaned in the doorway, "How many passengers are you going to have?" he asked. "Oh, five or six," I replied. "You better hope you CAN get out of here," he said. "Why is that?" I asked. "Last summer John Travolta's Lear almost took out the whole fence at the

147

end of the runway. He took off and he was too heavy," he replied. Needless to say, I didn't feel real comfortable until we cleared that mother and were headed toward Little Rock.

A Cowboys victory in their first post-season trip since 1985. I'm thankful it wasn't Lear One Dallas Cowboys last trip.

41

A LITTLE R&R

After the Cowboys 38-6 loss to the Detroit Lions in the 1991 N.F.C. divisional playoffs on January 5, 1992, Head Coach Jimmy Johnson had earned some well deserved rest and relaxation. He needed beaching, sunning, gambling and fishing. Nassau had it all, Jimmy and his family headed south for the Bahamas.

Jerry gave Jimmy and his girlfriend, Rhonda Rookmaaker, and his sons Brent and Chad, the use of Lear One Dallas Cowboys. That was their vacation and Jimmy's chance to get away from the pressures of head coaching in the National Football League. It was also a rare opportunity for him to get away from Jerry, even if it was only for four days.

By now the writing was on the wall, Jimmy Johnson had things headed in the right direction. "I'm doing whatever the hell I want to do," he said. That meant: Coaching the Cowboys, drinking Heineken's, eating ribs, counting cards and living alone in his big house. The saltwater fish aquariums and their contents were his ideal companions.

There were no pets, no wife and no kids around. His sons Brent, then 28, and Chad, 26, were more like friends. They seemed closer than ever. Jimmy was performance-oriented, fiery and extremely competitive by nature. Everyone knew that. He always wanted to be judged by how well his team played on any given Sunday.

I can honestly say, if his sons were second on his list of importance behind winning football games, as had been reported, then it had to have been taken completely out of context. If Chad and Brent supposedly trailed coaching football by a wide margin, I would have noticed. The man I came to know, and the man that everyone thought they knew, was not the same man the team knew during the rigors of an entire season in the National Football League.

When Jimmy was away from football, if only for a few days, he was a very relaxed, friendly and kindhearted person. He was always nice to me and I genuinely liked, respected and admired him. I still do. On scouting trips, and the other numerous trips when he was onboard, we always had a lot of fun with Jimmy.

I always thought it was interesting that whenever a reporter interviewed or commented on Jimmy's selfish lack of interest in his family, they always asked his eldest son, Brent. He displayed absolutely no interest whatsoever in the Dallas Cowboys, or for that matter, the game of football. If the same set of questions had been answered by my friend, and Jimmy's youngest son, Chad, the answers would have been decidedly different. Chad was a regular fixture at every home game and most of the Cowboys away games.

They had been in Nassau for a day or two when Jimmy arranged a charter for a deep sea fishing trip the following day. It was a great day at the pool. We had a few Heinekens, listened to reggae and relaxed. Jimmy said, "Todd, if you want to go deep sea fishing with us tomorrow morning, meet us down in the lobby around six."

That was very early in the afternoon. I was excited when I spoke to Eddy about the offer. "Todd, this is their vacation, Jimmy works hard all year long and he wants to be with his family. He was probably just saying that to be nice," Eddy said. He asked me not to go. I believed Eddy was upset because Jimmy didn't invite him.

Chad was my age. He and I went to dinner that evening, had a few drinks and gambled some. We sat down at the Blackjack tables with Jimmy and that is where the similarities ended. We weren't nearly as successful as Jimmy. It was uncanny. I watched in amazement as his win-loss ratio rapidly exceeded his record at the University of Miami—52-9.

A short time later, Jimmy decided it was time for a break. We headed in the direction of the Carnival Crystal Palace's only dance club, "Fanta Z." On display in the casino, was a brand-new bright red Cadillac Allante' convertible. It boasted a window sticker of almost $60,000. Jimmy stopped, turned to Rhonda and asked, "Would you like to have it? I've got enough chips in my hand to buy it for you." He was dead-serious. He would have purchased it for her on the spot.

Chad and I stayed at "Fanta Z" until the wee-hours of the morning. We weren't very good gamblers, but luck was with us. After chasing, and successfully catching a couple of good-looking tourists, we were on our way to the rooms. As we stepped off the elevator Chad said, "You're going fishing with us tomorrow, you'd better get some sleep." The four of us laughed at the innuendo. "I don't think so," I replied. "Why not?" he asked. "Eddy doesn't think I should," I said. "Todd, if my dad didn't want you to go with us, he wouldn't have invited you. If you want to go, you are more than welcome to," Chad replied. It was decision time.

I went. I rolled out of bed which was not an easy task for two obvious reasons. First of all, she was wonderful. Secondly, it was 5:30 a.m. One of the few things that made the job bearable were the once in a lifetime opportunities like that. Why couldn't I go fishing with Jimmy Johnson and his family?

We had a great time. I was in a heap of trouble with the chief pilot when I returned, however. Eddy figured I had bucked his authority. As everyone boarded the airplane at Sky Harbour Aviation at Nassau's International Airport for departure the following day, Jimmy told Eddy, "I invited Todd, I wanted him to go...." It helped some when Jimmy spoke up for me like that. Some.

Jimmy Johnson, of all people, knew how easy it was to step off the management sidewalk and onto the grass. He knew that appropriate action guidelines were not always followed by Cowboys management and it seldom made any difference how minor the infraction may have been. He helped to ease the tension.

Fortunately, for the rest of the NFL, winning with the Cowboys proved considerably tougher than winning at Blackjack. All Jimmy conceded he needed to do before they headed into the 1992 season was plug in a couple of blue-chip players and he knew they would win. Several Heinekens later "We will win a few Super Bowls...." he said. "Then I'm gonna go lie on the beach for the rest of my days," he loudly proclaimed.

Jimmy was absolutely right. He won his first of two Super Bowls just over a year later. He won his second almost one year after that. Unlike Jerry, Jimmy always spoke the truth and he always kept his word. All that was needed for him to accomplish his goals was a little help from his friend, Jerry Jones. He promptly moved back to Miami just like he said he would.

Life's a beach....

42

THE VOICES

On any given weekend in early spring, and throughout most of the summer, it was very unusual for Lear One Dallas Cowboys not to be parked on the ramp at Miracle Strip Aviation in beautiful Destin, Florida. Destin is the proud home of one of the nation's best deep sea fishing rodeos and is a wonderful place to visit. Jerry Jones often retreated to his exclusive and private beachfront home, it was a workaholics paradise. It was also his favorite place to escape with family, friends or girlfriends.

With the schedule that we kept, it was also a very well deserved semi-rest for an often exhausted flight crew. Eddy and I departed one early April afternoon for a weekend in Destin. We flew to Little Rock, picked up Charlotte and Shy, and continued on to our destination. As we left the vestiges of winter far and quickly behind, we welcomed the warmth of the Florida panhandle sun. No harbinger warned us of the horror to come.

Jerry Jones and the "New Regime"

On April 19, 1992, our departure day, Eddy was lying on his stomach watching television in his hotel room. Apparently, when he got up to start getting dressed and ready for the flight home, he pulled something in his back. He was bent over in pain and could barely walk. I encouraged him to tell Jerry but he did not want the family to know. Oh, they could see that he was in pain, but I don't think they knew the extent of his injury. I don't think Eddy realized the extent of his injuries.

We were supposed to leave at noon. Nothing was ever "scheduled." It was at least four or five hours later when we were finally onboard the airplane and headed for Dallas. The weather was reported by flight service as extremely severe to the north and northeast of the Dallas area, however, following our flight plan route would put us far enough to the south and possibly behind the storm.

Eddy was miserable. He was dead tired and in pain. Meanwhile, Al was permanently on leave. The flight crew had taken more hits than an All-Pro and somehow managed not to drop the ball. We sacrificed our interests and time and any semblance of a normal life. Why? To ensure the timely and safe transportation of the most prominent owner in professional sports and his most prized cargo—his entire family.

It is one thing when a pilot flies tired. It is another thing to fly tired AND be physically unable to perform your flight duties. Whether for the job or his need to get Jerry Jones back to Dallas, Eddy was determined to catch the red-eye to Little Rock that night to see his doctor. During midflight, they decided to fly into Little Rock first to drop off Charlotte's husband, Shy. Eddy should have said, "I am in serious pain and the weather is terrible. Let's just go to Dallas, Shy and I can take the late night flight back to Little Rock." It should have been a go or no-go situation call from the captain.

My gut feeling was... "Don't." Our flight plan route from Little Rock to Dallas showed level five out of a possible six in the thunderstorm department. Severe embedded thunderstorms, possible tornadoes, hail and cloud to cloud lightning were also reported. Flight service provided a lengthy list of convective SIGMETs, aviation jargon for significant meteorological activity. Significant was an understatement.

I double checked the weather in Dallas and along our planned route of flight. I listened to flight service's recommendations. I also knew my captain was flying tired, in pain, and we would be flying into known severe weather. I thank God I'm still alive today to wonder: WHY?

The weather had deteriorated. We shot an instrument approach into Little Rock, barely making it. Our drop off of Shy was complete, additional fuel was onboard and a poor decision had been made. Jerry Jones wanted to go to Dallas...tonight. Eddy said he would attempt to fly that last leg due to the seriousness of the weather. Please, be my guest.

It was BAD! REAL BAD! Everyone has experienced air pockets while inflight, they are normally not serious. These were serious! We were literally dropping over 2,000 feet per second, PER SECOND! Up, then down, up and down. We were forced violently to and fro by the unstable air, it was impossible to maintain a constant altitude. We asked for a block altitude of 4,000 feet. Under normal conditions, flight levels and altitudes are 2,000 feet apart. Our color radar confirmed the nightmare, it was solid red—level six thunderstorms and we were right in the middle of it.

The very few commercial airliners in the sky that night were also trying desperately to avoid the powerful storms. The heightened sense of awareness and concern was definitely evident in all of our voices that night. "Center, this is American 632, we need an immediate...immediate 30 degree right turn for weather." "Delta 4011, I need a 40 degree left turn now!"

Air traffic control tried to accommodate everyone to the best of their capabilities, without letting us fly into each other. That was not an easy task under those conditions. A charter aircraft based at Dallas' Love Field reported a direct lightning strike, rendering its onboard color radar useless. At night, with pouring rain, monstrous thunderstorms and no radar, they could have flown directly into the maelstrom. They had no way to "see", talk about a wing and a prayer.

Meanwhile, everyone in the back was yelling, screaming and crying—yes, crying. "Please, turn around. Let's go back, go back!" they screamed. We had already gone through the gates of hell. If we turned around we would have had to do it all over again. We were not going back...Period. My teeth literally chattered from the impact. Our navigation and flight instruments were virtually unreadable on the panel. They were a constant blur of lights.

We circumnavigated the thunderstorms and tried to hit the soft spots, and we held on, tight. The fasten seat belt sign was never turned off and if they were moving free around the cabin, it was not by choice! The northeastern side of the Dallas area looked and appeared to be the softest spot. Eddy and I headed in that direction. It was not better...it was much worse. I told Eddy, "We cannot go that way!" I was navigating, communicating and monitoring the radar, giving him instructions to turn left, then right. Eddy was just trying to keep the wheels down and the shiny side up.

Gene was close to tears. Karen, Stephen's wife, was in tears and screaming in the back. Pitch black and with lightning popping all around us, hail joined the heavy, heavy, rains. It was so violent I thought the wings would be ripped from the airplane. As I looked up from our lifesaving radar, I caught a glimpse of our airspeed indicator. We were concentrating so intensely on keeping our wings level when I realized that we were almost at normal cruise speed, Mach .80.

"What are you doing, Eddy?" I asked. With the frightening force of those thunderstorms, if we had flown into one of those huge thunderclouds at that speed, we would all be recollections and memoirs. The radar was painted completely red; the voices were tinged with fear. "Eddy, pull the power back. Slow down!" I said. He did not respond. "Get back to maneuvering speed. You are going to tear the wings off this thing!" I screamed. With no all-important crew coordination going on at that point, I called Center.

"Fort Worth Center this is Lear One Dallas Cowboys. Give us a heading for Shreveport...immediately," I said. The young co-pilot had just taken over the flight. Center reported that it looked a little better toward that direction. No one had actually tried that route, so they asked us to give them a pilot report. We were only 80 miles away from Shreveport. Only ten more flight minutes and we would be out of this hell hole.

"What are you doing?" Eddy's voice was pitched higher than usual. "Eddy, we can't go to the northeast. We cannot make the Blue Ridge Arrival. We are not going that way,"

I firmly replied. "Well, we are only about 80 miles outside of Shreveport, let's give it a try," he agreed.

Jerry still wanted to turn around; it was another do or die situation. We gingerly made our way toward Shreveport and joined the Scurry Arrival, our original plan, and continued on to Dallas. That routing became the only way into Dallas that night. As we taxied up to the familiar signs of Jet East, everyone was ghost white. For the first time, not one word was spoken. Complete silence.

I helped Eddy out of the cockpit and watched as he hobbled across the tarmac and into a Jet East courtesy van. He headed to Dallas/Fort Worth International Airport for American Airlines red-eye home to Little Rock. Eddy was on his way, set to go back through everything we had just experienced, only this time he was a passenger.

Two days later, while Eddy prepared for back surgery, I received a phone call from my captain. "Todd, I have flown with many, many pilots. You are young, but you are one of the best weather pilots I have ever flown with," he said. "To tell you the truth, that flight back to Little Rock was the first time I was ever in an airplane when I really felt as if we weren't going to make it. My back was hurting so bad that I really didn't even care."

Then, he thanked me.

43

THE RIVER

It scared the ever-living shit out of everyone in the back, and front, when they were suddenly thrown from their seats. Food and drinks flew everywhere. Washington National Tower asked, "Lear One Dallas Cowboys, are you going to be able to make your landing?" In aviation the goal is to retire with the same number of landings as takeoffs. Like Jerry Jones always said, "Shit'll do for brains, if you're lucky." We were real lucky.

It happened during the almost three months time when Eddy was on hiatus while recuperating from back surgery. Al, my favorite captain, was on permanent leave at home in Little Rock taking care of his critically ill wife. I became interim chief pilot flying Jerry's bruising schedule, with "loaner" pilots from Jet East's charter department. Captain David Fabian made the trip to Washington, D.C., with me that day.

The Joneses departed Little Rock on May 22, 1992, and were flying to Georgetown University for Jerry, Jr.'s graduation ceremonies. Jerry and Gene, Shy and

Charlotte, Stephen and Karen, and Mrs. Chambers, Gene's mother, were onboard. They seldom, if ever, wore their seat belts like they were supposed to. The fasten seat belt sign was turned on but without a flight attendant in the back, who would make sure the boss buckled up? I'm a Learjet pilot, not a babysitter.

Not unlike other airports all across the country on a clear VFR day, when flying into D.C., approach control assigned the River Visual Approach. Follow the traffic in front, maintain adequate spacing, and wind in and out following the Potomac River to the airport. It was the scenic route.

We were cleared by approach control to 3,000 feet and instructed to contact National Tower. "Lear One Dallas Cowboys, maintain visual separation with traffic, you're number two. You are cleared to land Runway 18," Tower replied. We were cleared to land behind a Boeing 737.

In the meantime, that same 737 was taking a long, slow and lazy approach. Much slower than a normal approach speed. They were flying so slow, it looked to me as if the airplane seemed to be backing up. We kept gaining ground, actually air, getting closer and closer behind them. They were down and dirty, meaning, the landing gear and flaps were down in full landing configuration. I guess they were enjoying the scenery more than we were.

We had to descend and cross certain points along the arrival route at F.A.A. published and recommended altitudes. Behind that 737, swirling winds from the big boy came off of his wing tips. They were small versions of tornadoes. We needed to make sure they were below our intended flight path so those vortices would dissipate downward and not affect us, we hoped.

The River

Traffic into Washington National was always heavy and that 737 was going so slow they were impossible to avoid. At 1,200 feet we were on final approach when we hit the right vortice. Lear One Dallas Cowboys rolled 90 degrees up on its side, completely vertical. Our airspeed decreased instantly; we were going to stall!

Dave was on the controls as pilot in command. I grabbed my co-pilot's controls and the two of us tried to fight it. Dave threw full power to 1DC in an attempt to salvage some critical airspeed. We knew that we had just encountered the left vortice as we rolled the other way, not quite as severe at maybe 30 to 45 degrees. They were definitely attention grabbers and not much fun.

We did land because I'm still here to tell the story. A small commuter aircraft attempted to land on crossing Runway 21, they executed a go-around because that same 737 was in the way as the commuter was landing. They enjoyed the scenery on the ground, too, it appeared. All of this happened about the same time that the food and passengers in the back started flying on their own.

It had been a real life or death situation. There was simply no room to spare at such a low altitude. Plus, we had one hell of a time just getting the Lear under control and stabilized. We gained almost 500 feet in altitude from the turbulent rolls. The good news was that we didn't go head first into the Potomac River from 1,200 feet. The bad news was that we were caught in a 737s wake.

A bellow from the back wanted to know, "Jesus Christ! What the hell happened?" I described it as a wake because Jerry was not hands-on when it came to flying. Unlike everything else, his office was in the back and ours was in the front. It just did not seem like the right time to explain vortices and cyclonics. Everyone, myself included, was a little shaken up.

As we deplaned at the Butler Aviation terminal, the questions began. "What the hell did you say happened?" Jerry asked again. Dave chimed in with, "Yeah, we caught some wake from the 737 in front of us." Jerry left it at that and never mentioned it again. Dave looked at me and said, "I've never been through anything like that before."

All I could say was, "Neither have I, Dave. Neither have I."

44

HE'S NOT SHY ANYMORE

Captain Dave Fabian worried and expressed some concern to me about the incident in Washington, D.C. He was the "loaner" pilot from Jet East that flew the majority of flights with me during Eddy's extended stay on injured reserve. He wanted to know if Jerry had ever said anything about that turbulent approach into Washington National that almost put us head first into the Potomac. Everyone wants approval, and even though it was not his fault, he was naturally concerned.

I assured him that everything was fine. Maybe he was simply feeling insecure and nervous. During Eddy's absence, I had flown with virtually every captain that Jet East employed. Steve Blake, Gene Daigneault, Terry Klotz, Arlie Long, and Fabian. They were all nice fellas. That was his first flight with Jerry and the Joneses since everyone had tumbled out of their seats in Washington a few weeks before.

We were prepared to leave for Little Rock when he asked a simple question, "Todd, are these people nice?"

Although he had flown numerous flights for Jerry he was seldom, if ever, acknowledged for his efforts. The Cowboys were truly a thankless organization. Jerry Jones often seemed to make one feel as if we should feel privileged to wait at airports for them. By then, I thought I knew most of the Joneses habits and idiosyncrasies inside and out. I thought wrong.

"They are nice. You won't have any problems. Just be yourself, do your job and I guarantee you'll enjoy it," I said. I never learned. I was glad I had finally found someone to fly with that was fun to be around on the road. Someone that would actually leave their hotel room. I told Dave how much fun we were going to have in Florida and how much I enjoyed going there. It was time to relax on the beach. We departed Dallas and flew to Little Rock to pick up Charlotte and Shy.

Shy and Charlotte had married one year earlier. Slowly but surely, I had noticed changes in the now very, very rich Mr. Anderson. As we loaded the Joneses always overstuffed luggage at Central Flying Service that summer day in 1992, everyone was inside the terminal ready for Destin. Shy walked out to the airplane with his golf clubs. It was always a mess when they brought their golf clubs. We never had enough room for their luggage, much less....

Actually, the family had far outgrown Lear One Dallas Cowboys. Too many people, too many play things, and too much luggage. They were simply too much for the Lear. The only place to put those dreaded golf clubs was in the aisle. Not exactly the safest place for them, but I certainly never told them what to take or not to take on their vacations. That was an item of little concern.

He's Not Shy Anymore

I was in the airplane hastily rearranging luggage in hopes of getting it all in. Shy walked up to Dave. "You again. Hopefully, you can load luggage better than you can fly," Shy said. He dropped those golf clubs right in Dave's face, turned around and walked back toward the terminal. I really wish he had just handed them to him. I stepped out of the door at about that time. Dave was standing there looking down at the clubs lying at his feet.

"What an asshole," Dave screamed. "He's normally not like that, what happened, was it an accident?" I asked. "No, Todd. He dropped them right in front of my face," Dave replied. I could tell that really offended Dave. I reached down and picked them up. I was embarrassed for Dave, for the Joneses, and for myself. I wanted so badly to inform Shy that maybe he needed to attend the same school of public relations Jerry had attended during the past few years.

Shy had never acted like that before. He used to sit in the front near the cockpit and shoot the shit with us. That time he stepped in it. All I could figure was the money had changed him. It affects some people like that. One minute they fit their britches and the next second they are way too big for 'em. Come to think of it, I guess once he found his seat in the back, he was now certifiably one of them. Everyone else was now far beneath him.

Dave never complained about any of the Joneses. He did a great job of filling in for the injured Lear Cowboys and I appreciated it. None of the Jet East pilots that I flew with during Eddy's hiatus ever complained about the final destinations that we frequented. They let their feelings be known, however, that trying to get there was a completely different story. They were right. Each and every one of them were thrilled when Eddy finally returned.

From the outside looking in, they saw things as they really were. They never noticed the Dallas Cowboys helmet on the tail. The countless hours of work, not to mention the relentless and frenzied pace, was taking its toll. Things are not always as they sometimes seem. I was proud to be a part of the Dallas Cowboys. Unfortunately, working for Jerry Jones often required everyone to swallow their pride and bite their tongues. Dave flew for less than three months and he had seen enough.

I never thought it would happen. The lust from the logo had begun to fade. Forever.

45

LIGHTEN UP!

Jerry Jones and his family, in private, talked about everyone in the Cowboys organization. It kept them entertained. "Best Friend" Jimmy Johnson and his staff, Tommy Hodges, then President of Texas Stadium Corporation and Joel Finglass, Director of Ticket Sales and Promotions were frequent targets. Even insiders and members of Jerry's "Arkansas Mafia" like 'Gorgeous' George Hays, the Cowboys Vice-President and Director of Marketing, was not immune. His ears must have burned on a daily basis.

It was never enough. Jerry could always do it better and he made sure that everyone was well-aware that if they couldn't do it, someone else would. Jerry's comments "off the record and between us girls" were never constructive, they always seemed threatening. If he had only known how many "Jerry Stories" routinely ran the grapevine.

I noticed immediately, however, that blood was truly thicker than water and Jerry always took care of his own.

It never stopped them from teasing one another, however. Just like any other family, the relatives were fair game. Of special interest was Gene's younger sister, Trish.

She was known throughout the Jones family for having a slightly bitchy side to her. I never really noticed it, she seemed to blend in real well. On that particular flight, however, she became the butt of their jokes because of the way she finally decided to relax and take some of the edge off. Jerry Jones never condemned anyone for behavior along those lines. He relieved his stress in the same manner, on more than one occasion, in the back of Lear One Dallas Cowboys. It gets my vote, too.

Trish was seeing Jack Dixon. He was a long-time associate of Jerry's, the Cowboys Treasurer and 'Mafia' member. Eddy and I were waiting at Jet East when she and Jack arrived at the airport for their flight to Little Rock. Apparently, they could not contain themselves any longer. The gig was up when everyone saw them putting their clothes back on and regaining their composure as they exited the back seat of the taxicab.

We always thought that Trish and Jack seemed a strange pair. We had our theories. Perhaps, Gene had finally realized that she owned everything from the 20 yard line north. Trish was a simple way for her to keep an eye on Jerry's money. The platinum card bills certainly did not arrive at their home address. Jerry was a firm believer in blood is thicker than water. Looked like Gene may have believed in it, too.

Gene could not believe her sister's behavior, however. They teased Gene and Trish during the entire flight. They said things like, "Mother, in case you haven't noticed, Trish seems a whole lot nicer than normal today, doesn't she?" they poked. "Trish, you don't seem as edgy today. You kind of took the edge off, didn't you?" They laughed the entire flight. The family was never threatened, only teased. By that time, I had overheard far too many private conversations in the back of the Learjet. The only thing that ever really changed, however, were the names of the innocent. That list grew smaller by the second.

Jerry believed that if he could own, preside and manage the most valuable franchise in professional sports: The Dallas Cowboys—not to mention international oil and gas production companies; oversee his interests in banking, real estate, crude oil shipping, refining and poultry processing; satisfy his passions for hunting and entertain his mistresses—then by God surely they could coach a football team, sell a few season tickets or a couple of luxury suites at Texas Stadium.

His 550 mph attitude and two hours sleep per night, had begun to wear him down. I was not surprised when I learned that he took handfuls of medication for his heart condition. At the very least it proved that he did, in fact, have one. He had been diagnosed with arrhythmia. Jerry had an irregular heartbeat. He desperately needed to do one thing.

Jerry, lighten up!

46

LONDON CALLING

I still find it hard to believe the same Jerry Jones that would not let us have his leftover food scraps on the flight from Calgary to Detroit for the Lions game, was the same Jerry Jones whose wife left $30,000 in the safe deposit box at their London hotel. Completely forgot about it. Never even missed it. Had it not been for the concierge calling several months later, I guess Jerry would still be $30,000 short.

During the summer of 1992, Jerry and Gene were headed to London, England, for vacation. Marylyn usually tried to coordinate all of their flights, however, she was going to be out of pocket for this one. Eddy and I flew Jerry and Gene to New York's John F. Kennedy International Airport. They boarded the 1,350 mile per hour Concorde for their trip across the Atlantic and we flew Lear One Dallas Cowboys back to Dallas.

Gene said they weren't exactly sure what day they were coming home. Although they had our phone numbers, Eddy wrote down his 1-800 satellite beeper number on the back of one of his business cards and handed it to Gene. She would call and let us know the day before they left London so we could be there to meet them when they arrived. It was only a five hour flight on the S.S.T. from London to New York. We thought the Lear was fast....

On the day of their departure they were in the hotel lobby and headed to Heathrow Airport. Gene suddenly remembered that she needed to call and let us know that they were on their way. She was supposed to have called the day before they left, but she forgot that minor detail. She paged Eddy and we headed to J.F.K. We met their arriving flight with time to spare. After they cleared customs, we went to the General Aviation terminal and headed home. No problem.

A few months later, Eddy and I were at Jet East when Marylyn called. The concierge from the hotel where they had stayed in London called to Valley Ranch and asked to speak with Eddy Collins. Of course, we were never there. We were always one of two places, in the air or at the airport. He apparently asked enough questions and somehow managed to get through the switchboard operator to Marylyn.

It seemed Gene had left $30,000 in the safe deposit box at their hotel suite in England. Yes, that's correct, $30,000. She never called to claim it, they had simply forgotten it. The poor lad did not know what to do with the money. They never called and requested it. Nothing. In her hasty rush to leave the hotel that day, after she remembered to call us, she left Eddy's card on the counter.

Jerry and Gene Jones flew in their private Learjet to New York. They comfortably sat in the fastest commercial airliner in the world, the Concorde. Seats were

$5,000 per person. A week was spent in one of London's poshest hotels. To top it all off, they left many of the Cowboys overworked employees entire yearly salary in a safe deposit box. For someone that seemed so financially shrewd, I always wished I had the money that Jerry and Gene "wasted" on a daily basis. I would have been rich.

One thing is for sure, he doesn't spend it for decent cups to drink out of at Texas Stadium!

47

GUNS AND GAUNTLETS

Veterans, rookies, superstars and waiver wires. Coaches, fans, sponsors and hordes of news media. An owner, contracts, holdouts and short tempers. Curfews, condoms, titty bars and bullshit. Food, fun, guns and gauntlets. It was all of the above and so much more, deep in the heart of Texas. The practices were free but Jerry Jones could have charged a fee for the antics off the field. The Dallas Cowboys were in training camp.

Bruce Mays had been with Jimmy Johnson for 14 years. He was former Associate Athletic Director at the University of Miami. When Jimmy Johnson abruptly left to become Head Coach of the Dallas Cowboys, Bruce came to Texas with him. As Director of Operations and Football Facility Coordinator, Bruce had one tough job trying to keep the organization coordinated, operated, facilitated and directed. Impossible is the one word that comes to mind. Bruce somehow managed to make the impossible...possible.

It was his work during training camp in Austin in 1992 that almost did him in, however. Everything from the arrangement of the best hotels and transportation for the Cowboys players and staff while on the road, to the most minute special requests or details, Bruce, Craig Glieber and Steve Carichoff took care of everything. They took it all in stride.

Bruce and his staff were also in charge of handling the food at training camp, for the entire duration of camp. No small feat in itself. Eddy and I watched with amazement one afternoon as a 6'7", 311 pound offensive tackle, named Kevin Gogan, drank 16 large glasses of fruit punch, Gatorade, water and orange juice. Not in one day, Kevin accomplished that feat at lunch! They simply should have stocked up.

Anyone with an official "pass" ate every meal free of charge. Players and staff were on one side of the cafeteria at St. Edwards University. News media, reporters, select visitors, sponsors, etc., sat on the other. I didn't think the food was that bad but I was in and out of camp on a daily basis it seemed. I also didn't sweat through practice in 100 degree temperatures everyday, sleep in dorm rooms every night or eat the same foods over and over again in the cafeteria. It was inevitable—the players began to complain, and complain, and complain.

They were fed up with the endless array of noodles at St.Edwards. I overheard offensive tackle Mark Tuinei tell Troy Aikman "I've got your noodle...right here," as they moved through the chow line. The last straw came one week prior to the end of camp, however. During breakfast they, uh, ran out of milk. Jimmy Johnson, being funny, decided one morning that his old pal Bruce must pay for the unpardonable sin of sorry food at the old chuckwagon. Mays was ordered to run the gauntlet. Everyone has seen the old movies, and not so old commercials, where disgruntled cowboys threatened to hang the cook. Try running the gauntlet.

The gauntlet—even the name sounds menacing. Jimmy lined up ten big dummies with pads, ten full-sized Cowboys on each side of the line. He assumed the players would take it easy on good ol' Bruce. "I thought they'd nudge him and everyone would get a laugh out of it," Jimmy said. "They used those things to beat the hell out of Bruce." They almost put him in the hospital. Picture this, ten guys average size 280 pounds, knocked him from side to side and slammed him down on the ground. Honestly, they beat the ever-living shit out of him.

Bruce was real upset about being beaten to a pulp. Jimmy was upset; he had no idea that Mays would get the same gauntlet normally reserved for a player about to be placed on the waiver wire. But he did. I guess there might be something to those old movies. It just didn't pay to come between a Cowboy and good grub.

Only Jerry Jones would have picked the Capitol of Texas as the new home for Cowboys training camp in the first place. It wasn't Austin's centralized location, accessibility or deep-heated promise of conditioning that led him there. The players would learn to like it or else. Why? The move from Thousand Oaks saved Jerry and his purse strings over $400,000 per year. There was never a dull moment in or around Austin and St. Edwards University when the Dallas Cowboys were in town. Lets see now, where shall I begin....

Eddy and I flew former Washington Redskin, seven year veteran and holdout defensive tackle, Dean Hamel, to Austin during his contract dispute with management, i.e. Jerry and Jimmy. On that hot August morning in 1991, when we arrived at Page AvJet, Eddy and I offered to give Dean a ride to St. Edwards.

As we drove up to Premont Hall, the players' dormitory, Dean, better known as "The Tasmanian Devil" promptly told Jimmy Johnson that "I'd like to tear your head off!" The reason? A strong '91 draft had produced number 1 pick, Russell Maryland, and the raw talent of Leon Lett. Both were in camp. Dean reacted to Johnson's remark that maybe "He'd better stick to golf...." Dean owned the Cowboys Driving Range which is located about a Par-5 distance from Valley Ranch headquarters.

Jimmy was saved by the bell, however. The dinner bell, that is. It was lunch time so Dean decided to think about it over lunch. A free lunch provided for by management. Hmmmm. Dean probably wished he could have borrowed Kelvin Martin's gun.

Eleventh-round rookie running back from the University of Michigan, Tony Boles, looked up to Cowboys star Emmitt Smith. In front of Premont Hall one afternoon, I was in the parking lot talking to Number 22. Emmitt was retrieving several CD's from the rear of his Nissan Pathfinder. "Emmitt, can I borrow your truck for awhile? I'll gas it up for ya. Come on," Tony pleaded. "Well, okay. I know you won't need these," Emmitt teased. We laughed as he produced a twelve pack of condoms. "Rookies don't get no...."

Emmitt continued trash talking as he handed over his credit card. "This is for the gas," he said. Twenty-four hours later Emmitt reported both his truck and credit card stolen to the Austin police department. Two days later, Emmitt's truck was back, his credit card was back and Boles was back. Tony was fined $5,000 and his career was over. Emmitt probably wished he could have borrowed Freddie Childress' gun.

Several of the rookies and younger players often missed the 11:00 p.m. curfew and bed-check because they could not resist a tour of the local titty bars. It was a $450 fine for missing curfew. That was probably part of the reason that Bruce Mays had received such a beating that day he ran "The Gauntlet." He was Jimmy Johnson's henchman.

Jerry often broke Gene's curfew; he spent some time at "Sugars" himself. Now, that would have been a site to see, Jerry Jones and several of his newly signed rookies at "Sugars" all breaking curfew. I could imagine Jerry explaining, "Honey, I did it for team unity!" Gene, more than once, probably wished she could have borrowed anybody's gun.

Eddy and I stood on the sidelines one blazing 102 degree afternoon and chatted with Stephen Jones. Practice is practice, sweat is sweat and athletes are athletes, but HELLO! We had somehow managed to get caught downwind of Trinidad native and former Pitt Panther running back, Curvin Richards. Curvin was busy trying to become Emmitt's backup and the task obviously left no time for "Shower Time." His Cowboy teammates had finally persuaded him to take a shower...every three days. Two-a-day practices in 100 degree Austin heat. On that day, he had to have been at the very least, on his third day. I wished someone would have gotten me a gun.

Comments, criticism and bullshit were also the norm. I never heard so much. Coaches constantly told the players they were "looking good." Especially the character that lived inside the effervescent running backs coach Joe Brodsky. We heard him as he yelled at a no-name longshot one afternoon, "Looking good baby! Man you got a shot!" Then he looked over at Eddy, Jerry, Mike McCoy and I. Joe snickered and rolled his eyes.

The Cowboys were rebuilding...and reloading.

48

THE QUIET ASSASSIN

At the beginning of the 1992 season several of the Cowboys players were holding out because of contract disputes. That was, and still is, a regular occurrence in their salary negotiations with Jerry Jones. Professional football is simply another form of big business getting bigger, much bigger. The players may have played football, but Jerry signed the paychecks.

Cowboys training camp was in full swing. We were flying the "1DC Shuttle." We flew everyone and we flew often. The Cowboys had lost a few players to Plan B in 1992, most notably middle linebacker, Jack Del Rio, to the Vikings. Most of their draft picks were already signed, however. Contract talks were still in progress for several Cowboys starters and key veterans.

The contract talks in progress/holdout list included: Ray Horton, Michael Irvin, Jim Jeffcoat, Ken Norton, Jay Novacek, Vinson Smith, Mark Stepnoski, Tony Tolbert and James Washington. No trouble recognizing any of those names. Cowboys starting safety James

Washington and Jerry had finally agreed to terms. James flew in from California and signed. He was a Cowboy for one more year.

Upon arrival at Jet East on the afternoon of August 11, 1992, James and I were sitting on the ramp in Lear One Dallas Cowboys waiting to depart for Austin. We knew that Jerry was on his way to the airport. "Go ahead and get our clearance so we can be ready to go when he gets here. Take care of James," Eddy said. I received our takeoff clearance from Tower and sat back for a little conversation with the "head hunter."

James Washington rarely talked to reporters or the media, he usually kept to himself. James preferred to let his aggressive play on the football field speak for him. We small talked while we waited for Jerry to arrive. Every player that we flew, and we flew a lot of them, were always as nice as the day was long.

We talked about the airplane. Everyone seemed to always have questions about the airplane. James talked about his family in Los Angeles. He mentioned that he had been teammates with Troy Aikman, Frank Cornish and Ken Norton when he was in college. U.C.L.A. was a white boy's paradise with all of those beautiful California girls, James said. I told him that I had a fondness for a couple of Raiderettes but Texas wasn't too far behind.

We talked about how Jerry didn't want to pay him. He was glad to finally be signed and relieved it was all behind him. James remarked that Jerry certainly was a hard negotiator and he really didn't know if he would end up playing for the Cowboys that year or not. Make no mistake about it, he wanted to. Jerry, however, made it seem like he could take it or leave it. "That's his style," I confirmed.

The Quiet Assassin

Suddenly, the conversation shifted, it was deja vu. Jerry Jones and his "yes men" seemed to have developed a disconcerting trend. The interesting part of his questions was that they were almost identical to the ones made by former Viking, Cowboy, Falcon and current Miami Dolphin linebacker, Jesse Solomon.

I didn't place much value on Jesse's remarks, he was unhappy to begin with. James, however, was a Cowboys starter. Last season he had finished second on the team in tackles and lead all defensive backs with 113 bruising stops. He was a crowd favorite and a key contributor in the secondary.

In the past, I had been well versed on Emmitt and his struggles with Jerry and his wallet. I had engaged in a very long conversation on this subject with Jesse Solomon two years prior. I set Jesse straight and simply chalked that up to bitterness. James Washington, however, was not bitter.

It seemed apparent that the black players felt that Jerry treated them unfairly. Not because of his "business is business" bottom-line callousness, but because they were black. "I'm not the only one that feels this way, some things are gonna have to change around here," James said.

The players were "real." They were the ones who played the game. I watched the Cowboys in person, week in and week out, at home and away. I viewed professional football quite differently now that I actually met and knew the owner, coaches and several of the players on the field. The fact remained that Jerry inevitably was called onto the proverbial carpet by the NAACP. As always, it had to be forced upon him. Jerry said things would change.

Apparently, we both had a lot to say. When Jerry finally arrived we had talked for almost one hour. We talked about life as we waited for Jerry—that never changed.

Things definitely have changed for the "wanna-be" Los Angeles Raider, James Washington. He is now a Washington Redskin.

49

NEVER AGAIN

It always revolved around the money. As long as Jerry Jones is in control of the Dallas Cowboys, it always will. Jerry has a lot of money and sometimes he'll spend it and sometimes he won't. The big misconception that many people seem to have is that every employee working for the Cowboys drives a Ferrari and lives in Highland Park. Hardly. The only person in the Cowboys organization that made any money was Jerry. Eddy learned a hard lesson about spending Jerry's money without his authorization.

Eddy had tried unsuccessfully for many months to get the flight crew on the same list with the coaches for uniforms. We were fortunate that we did not have to wear traditional pilot uniforms with ties and for that I was thankful. It was awfully hot on the ramp in the middle of a Texas summer. A Learjet cockpit consists of mostly glass windshield it was an oven in the front even with the air conditioning on. We dressed in the same golf shirts, slacks, sweaters and windbreakers as the coaching staff did. We looked good.

We flew so much, however, we quickly went through some threads. Finally, we began looking like the real cowboys at the rodeo, rather than the "jet jockeys" that we were. Eddy went to the Pro Shop at Texas Stadium and charged several hundred dollars worth of apparel for the flight crew. We were long overdue. He purchased new shirts, sweatsuits, sharp looking sweaters and a new windbreaker for us. Maybe it was the Dallas Cowboys coffee mugs that he threw in. All I knew was, that little shopping spree threw Jerry into a mad rage.

"No one does that, don't you ever do that again and you are not to charge anything to the Cowboys without SPECIFIC approval from me, is that clear?" Jerry screamed. Eddy assumed it was okay and in the past it probably was. We were employees that wore uniforms and we needed some new ones. He thought wrong. Jerry knew where every penny went and those pennies were spent where and when he saw fit. That was how he accumulated so many of them. It was one ugly ass chewing.

After that happened Eddy was a little hesitant to mention anything about uniforms. We never did get on the list, either. He didn't hesitate to run an "end around" to get what he wanted, however. He was forced into it. In the Cowboys organization unless anyone spoke up and let someone know, they never received anything, not even a thank you. At training camp in the summer of 1992, Eddy saw a cap that he wanted. Not just any old cap but one of the special caps that had "Dallas Cowboys Training Camp-Austin 1992" embroidered on it.

Everyone prized those caps and put their initials in them to keep up with 'em. The caps weren't prized because of the embroidery on the front, they were valuable because without a cap in Austin in the summer, well.... One of the fellas that worked in video, Randy Tinsley, made a fatal mistake and left his unattended. Eddy "borrowed" it! They say when a fella does something once, it gets easier. If Eddy saw some t-shirts in a box, he picked them up. Hats, t-shirts and shorts, he stuffed them all in his bag.

The Dallas Cowboys are a business, and like any other business, the owner watches the pennies. Jerry Jones watches every penny....

50

EVERYONE BEWARE!

The players in the National Football League do not, I repeat, do not need to go butting heads with the owners. We flew several of them and I know that the owners take their "toys" very seriously. It seemed as though we flew to an owners meeting somewhere on a monthly basis. With the help of their handy little Internet computers, those "hoss traders" made many ungentlemanly agreements. Hell, it's their money and they are fond of keeping it that way. Especially Jerry Jones.

The end to the Freeman McNeil trial on September 8, 1992, was a picture perfect example of the players outsmarting themselves. Freeman was the New York Jets' veteran running back. He and seven other players: Mark Collins, Don Majkowski, Tim McDonald, Frank Minnifield, Niko Noga, Dave Richards and Lee Rouson, sued the NFL and challenged the leagues Plan B free-agency system. Although Freeman received nothing monetarily for his efforts, he succeeded in starting the ball rolling. The owners and their players had operated

Jerry Jones and the "New Regime"

the past five years without a collective bargaining agreement. The rules of the game were about to change.

The McNeil trial and the ramifications that would likely ensue from the verdict were a hot topic of conversation in the back of Lear One Dallas Cowboys. Media speculation was high concerning free-agency, the NFL draft, roster size, medical and pension plans, salary caps, etc. Jerry had become a very influential owner in the league. Jerry, Stephen and Mike McCoy spent countless hours in anticipation and speculation. They certainly believed that the current Plan B system was lawful. Jerry and Jimmy had virtually rebuilt the Cowboys by effectively using it to their advantage.

Jerry and his fellow owners are businessmen. They took whatever steps were necessary to ensure competitive balance in the NFL. Although the McNeil case went to a jury trial in Minneapolis, it represented a turning point and a step in the right direction. It didn't really make that much difference to the owners. They voted in a salary cap soon afterwards and each franchise's marquis players were virtually unaffected. They always made the money and now they would simply make more. Through creative financing a team could stay, for the most part, entirely intact. Jerry Jones liked the cap, he was a master at "creative" financing. It was the lesser-knowns that were hurt by their business decisions. There are approximately 1,400 players in the NFL. Name 50 of them.

I had seen the owners behavior before. The owners and coaches know almost everything there is to know about a player long before he ever enters the league. I sometimes wondered if anyone was home under those helmets. Eddy and I flew many scouting trips prior to the draft. Several years ago we flew to a renowned major university on the east coast. After arrival around 10:00 a.m., Jimmy and his coaching staff headed in the direction of the university. Eddy and I settled in, as usual, for our wait at the airport. Less than one hour later we were surprised when they arrived at the airport for departure. We certainly weren't prepared because we didn't expect them to return until sometime after lunch.

That particular player was scheduled to work out for the Cowboys coaching staff. Upon their arrival, he said that he would rather perform the drills after lunch. He was hungry. We had flown all the way there for a college senior to tell Jimmy Johnson and the Dallas Cowboys that he preferred to work out after lunch. That did not go over very well with the head coach. No, he would not work out for them after lunch, or ever, for that matter. Jimmy and staff arrived at the airport and told us they were through and ready to go. As we prepared to depart, another NFL owner, head coach and staff arrived. They taxied to the same terminal where we were parked.

They were there for the same reason that we were. The owner and head coach of that particular west coast team had flown an even farther distance than we had. As they deplaned he walked over to chat. "Hey Jimmy, how did the work outs go this morning?" the coach asked. "Well, he wouldn't run for me, he said he was hungry!" Jimmy replied. "You're kidding?" he said in disbelief. The other influential and well-known NFL owner walked over to say hello. He smiled and shook everyone's hand. I wondered if he had heard the coaches conversation; he definitely had.

"Excuse me, Jimmy, but did I hear you say that he didn't want to work out for you?" he asked. "Yeah, he was hungry," Jimmy replied. "Is that right? Well, he won't work out for us either! Let's go," he replied, angrily. They said their goodbyes and departed right after we did. I couldn't believe it. I had witnessed something that was downright shocking. The National Football League and its owners are a large business association and they seemed to be in collusion together, for now. Jerry, although a leader among his self-serving peers, often lamented that many owners didn't pull their respective weight.

I know that many will find it hard to believe but Jerry Jones was not the only owner in the National Football League in dire need of an attitude adjustment. Many of Jerry's peers were as ruthless, self-centered and cold-blooded as he was. The only difference was that they didn't own the one franchise that transcends all of sports—The Dallas Cowboys.

Some teams are simply better than others on a yearly basis. Was it coaching or a commitment to winning from the upper levels of management? Do the owners even really care who won or lost during their Sunday afternoon cash cows? That player never played a down in the NFL. He was black-balled.

Every professional football player should be thankful for the God-given ability and talent necessary to play a child's game and make hundreds of thousands, sometimes millions of dollars per year doing it. It seemed as though the owners were only motivated by the money. I felt the players didn't play the game because they loved it, they played because of the money, and only for a team that they deemed worthy of their services. The owners and players need each other. The owners did not become owners without years of business savvy and the players did not become professional, without the extraordinary ability to play. It is a two-way street.

The owners had the ability to make or break someone on a moments notice, no matter how talented or highly touted that player may be. Without a team or organization to play for, it is all for naught. The players deserve their fair share and both sides need to compromise in the future. The players are "free" to work for any organization that will take them on but when it's time to line up at the pay window, make that "free" to work for less money.

Jerry said it best, "I never expected to get a contract that I am happy with but the players shouldn't expect to get one that they're happy with either. That is what negotiations are all about. That is how you make a deal." Everyone needs to work together now and in the future. Jerry and his fellow owners know how to make a deal better than the players might expect.

I heard the most prominent owner in all of sports in the back on a daily basis. Jerry loves to win. Jerry will do anything to win. I predict it to be just a matter of time before Jerry will begin to step on other owners toes. He had the potential to become a bloody thorn in Paul Tagliabue's side, just like Al Davis was to former commissioner Pete Rozelle, in an all out effort to win, win, and win some more. In Jerry's own words "There is no such thing as a fair fight...."

Everyone beware! I predict that before it's all over, Jerry Jones will make Al Davis look like an angel....

51

PERFORMANCE AND PAYCHECKS

Jerry Jones was often the target of much fan discontent. The outcry was sometimes due in part to his contract disputes with Cowboys veterans, high-priced draft picks and cream of the crop free agents. Oftentimes, it was just because he was Jerry. I guess that they preferred 7-9, 3-10 and 1-15 seasons. Regardless of how well Jimmy and his staff drafted in April and despite the sheer quantity of top picks that they had managed to acquire, the process soon required that Jerry reach real deep into his black-gold lined pockets.

In the Landry-Schramm good 'ol days, several of the biggest names in Cowboys history skipped training camp. Randy White, Ed "Too Tall" Jones, Tony Dorsett and Everson Walls preferred not to attend during the 1980's. As soon as football fever hit, which in Dallas was everyday, it should not have been that unusual an occurrence for the diehards.

Lee Roy Jordan's holdout in 1973 guaranteed him, courtesy of Tex Schramm, a dubious distinction.

Jerry Jones and the "New Regime"

Schramm's personal vendetta assured that number 55 was never displayed as part of the Cowboys "Ring of Honor." The Cowboys holdout had become as much a part of a Texas summer as heat and a backyard barbecue. No one could remember a summer when there wasn't "at least one...."

As the "New Regime" headed into the 1992 season, negotiations with 11 unsigned free agents were still incomplete. It looked like another summer at camp discontent. In 1991, the list included defensive tackles Danny Noonan and Dean Hamel, defensive end Danny Stubbs, linebacker Jack Del Rio, guard John Gesek, tight end Steve Folsom and fullback Alonzo Highsmith. Offensive lineman Jeff Zimmerman proved to be the ultimate no-show. The Cowboys may still be unsure as to his whereabouts.

In 1990, linebacker Jesse Solomon, running back Emmitt Smith, wide receiver Alexander Wright and defensive tackle Jimmie Jones took extended vacations. The Cowboys planned overseas trip during camp in '92 played a small part of an even bigger problem. There were rumors that several notables would wait and sign after the August 2nd exhibition game against the Oilers in Tokyo. Jimmy had loudly voiced his opinion on that plan to Jerry on a flight three weeks prior. Eddy and I were the ones excited about the game in Japan. The reason? We weren't going.

Adding insult to injury, the most potentially turbulent set of contract negotiations in recent memory took place with young Stephen Jones, then 27 year-old team Vice President. He played the nasty game of give-and-take with stubborn agents. The Steve Endicotts, Richard Howells and Leigh Steinbergs soon placed their calls directly to him. Stephen was thrust into the fray after he had learned all Jerry felt he could from Cowboys Director of Player Personnel, Bob Ackles.

Stephen was greeted by 11 unsigned veterans without contracts. An offensive list that included the NFL's leading receiver "Playmaker" Michael Irvin, tight end Jay Novacek and center Mark Stepnoski. On defense it was more of the same. Ends Jim Jeffcoat and Tony Tolbert, Linebackers Ken Norton, Jr., and Vinson Smith. Defensive backs Ray Horton, James Washington and Bill Bates were not going to be in attendance either.

The negotiation process, and any other process, really had not changed much. Jerry always had the final say—always. Jerry liked to do anything and everything in a hurry. Patience seemed the only virtue that he lacked. There was no question about it—he had none. Period. The pressure was on and when Stephen promptly replaced Ackles on May 21, 1992, he replaced a man with 39 years of pro football experience. Stephen was well aware of the tighter public scrutiny.

Stephen did have one very distinct advantage, however. He came to the table well armed with the infinite knowledge of Jerry, Mike McCoy and Bob Ackles behind him. He had grown up with money his entire life. He had handled multi-million dollar oil and gas leases before. He had worked with figures that contained much higher dollar amounts than many of the ones he soon dealt with on a daily basis. He was accustomed to handling large sums of money. Occasionally, he had to balance his own checkbook.

Upon graduation from high school at Little Rock Catholic, Stephen, Charlotte and Jerry, Jr., each received a cool $1 million from dear old dad. When they graduated from college the same financial incentive package applied then, too. They each received an additional $1 million from good 'ol "Daddy Warbucks." I knew that several agents tried to take advantage of the young and inexperienced Stephen Jones. It was their duty as player representatives.

If the Dallas Cowboys players contracts ever contained a clause that paid them for performance and provided for incentives in the same manner as Jerry's kids were rewarded, a most unusual event could occur. It would become the newest rage since the recently devised and much despised, "Voidable years." For certain, the now familiar training camp "No Show" would be a thing of the past.

Leigh Steinberg are you listening?

52

EXCUSE ME, BUT...

At large family reunions in the South, it is not uncommon for perfect strangers to stop by and join in on all of the fun. Everyone just assumed that they were long-lost relatives. Eventually, the questions became difficult to answer and they were sized up for what they really were—imposters and freeloaders. It was too late by then, they had eaten the food and drank the wine. The friend of a friend, of a friend, routine worked on Jerry and Gene Jones, also.

In addition to the Cowboys, Jerry also owns Texas Stadium Corporation. A very lucrative part of his financial puzzle. Many owners would kill for the opportunity to capitalize on such an asset. TSC operates the stadium for the Dallas suburb of Irving. The ticket offices and the Cowboys Pro Shop are located at Texas Stadium.

Pro Seat was in charge of selling seat options. The "options" were specialized seating sold for Cowboys home games. They were priced from $2,500 to $15,000 per season. It was strictly a sales job and a salesperson earned commissions based upon them. Joel Finglass was the Cowboys Director of Ticket Sales and Promotions and former Cowboys running back Robert Newhouse also worked at Texas Stadium.

Similar to any other commissioned sales positions, some employees succeeded and others failed. One of them was an idiot. There was a fella that went to work for Pro Seat prior to the season. Of the 14 or so people employed by Pro Seat, he was number 14. The Cowboys opened their season on Monday, September 7, 1992, against the Washington Redskins. Jerry and Gene planned an enormous invitation-only soiree prior to the game. Eddy and I flew several famous people into Dallas for that red carpet affair. It was "A Star-Studded Event With Gene and Jerry Jones."

The party was in full swing, no one noticed when the fella arrived with his girlfriend. He had only been working for the Cowboys about three weeks. He and his girlfriend joined right in on the festivities. They mixed, mingled and rubbed elbows with the privileged. Jerry and Gene were busy entertaining their guests and never noticed them. When the party finally ended, a select few were invited to Jerry's luxury suite on the 50 yard line, located directly above the Cowboys "Ring of Honor." The couple went right along with them. He walked in and introduced himself as Troy Aikman's cousin, sat down, and ordered his first round of drinks. The girlfriend was impressed, no doubt.

There were a lot of very important guests and celebrities that needed the Joneses attention while everyone watched the game and hobnobbed. Meanwhile, the lowest person on the Cowboys totem pole sat there and enjoyed the game from the best seat in the house. Gene didn't know exactly what to do and she did not want to cause a scene. Finally, during halftime she needed some answers. She asked them to step outside the suite for a second. "Excuse me, but who are you?" Gene asked. The fantasy was over.

It was a simple misunderstanding. Just because he sold seat options didn't mean he had any.

53

HOW 'BOUT THAT LEARJET!

The now famous owner and his Learjet became well-known all across the United States and internationally for several reasons. One of which was because we flew more than any other corporate flight department. Another was because our flights were not limited to any one area of the country. The real reason was the unforgettable call letters...Lear One Dallas Cowboys.

I quickly found out why the Cowboys were called "America's Team" whenever we checked in on the airwaves with the various air traffic control centers across the country. The controllers always gave us our clearance and then some. We always attracted a lot of attention on the ground, as well as in the air. The name Dallas Cowboys meant something to everyone. It was amazing.

In one instance, Eddy and I were flying into Teterboro, New Jersey, for a New York Giants game when I called Center, "New York Center, this is Lear One Dallas Cowboys," I said, as always. "Lear One Dallas Cowboys?

Jerry Jones and the "New Regime"

Whose plane is that, Jimmy's or Jerry's?" Center asked. Believe it or not, many times it was assumed the airplane belonged to Jimmy Johnson. With the $$$ that he will command when he returns to coaching, he may be able to afford one.

"Center, we've got the owner onboard, it's his airplane," Eddy said. "Really? I want to talk to him," he replied. "Jerry, they want to talk to you," I turned around and said. "Who wants to talk to me?" Jerry asked, puzzled. "The controller in New York. He wants to talk to you," I replied. Jerry had never talked on the Lear radio before. In fact, he was rarely ever near the cockpit. I handed him my headset, turned up the interior speaker volume so he could hear, and he took the radio.

"This is Jerry Jones," he drawled. "Jerry, you actually have a couple of Cowboy fans up here in the tower. They want to tell you good luck at the game tomorrow. I can't say the same for myself; I'm a Giants fan!" he said. Jerry started in with his "Come to Jesus" way of speaking. "You know we have Cowboy fans all across the country. The New York fans have always been real good to us. I look forward to a real good game tomorrow," he said. "It's been nice talking to you Jerry...Go Giants!" Center answered. "Go Cowboys!" Jerry replied. He was smiling broadly. Life was good.

Another time, after a pre-season game in Kansas City against the Chiefs, everyone was excited after the Cowboys win. It never really mattered if it was pre-season or not. A victory was a victory. We departed Kansas City International and I called Departure Control. "Kansas City Departure, Lear One Dallas Cowboys, checking in at 2000 feet," I said. "Lear One Dallas

Cowboys—in the pre-season—you are cleared to 17,000," came the reply. He was obviously a big Chiefs fan and just wanted to give us some good-natured jabbing. It was great.

The Dallas Cowboys were not as popular in the nations capital, however. We flew to Washington, D.C., for a game against the Redskins, during the media uproar when the "real" American Indians were feeling offended and degraded. Several professional sports teams had, and still do have, names like Braves, Redskins, Warriors, and Blackhawks. Somewhere, fans were doing the "tomahawk chop" on a daily basis. Most players and team owners thought the names and logos were a compliment associated with brave and aggressive warriors.

The controllers recognized us immediately. I was on the radio with National Tower. "National Tower, Lear One Dallas Cowboys is with you on the approach," I said. "We don't want any Cowboys up here! You're in Redskin country," Tower replied. Al was funny but he had a very, dry sense of humor. "Hey! you guys know you can't say that...you guys are called the Washington Native Americans," Al replied. The controller laughed. "Maybe so, but we still don't want any Cowboys on our range," he said. We won anyway.

One night Eddy and I were flying our personal version of the red-eye with Jerry and the rest of the vampires onboard. It was late at night and we were enroute to Dallas. There was never much chatter on the airwaves at that time of the night. There were a few intermittent voices from the overnight freight flyers.

Jerry Jones and the "New Regime"

I checked in with Center, "Center, Lear One Dallas Cowboys with you, flight level three-three-zero," I said. Center replied with the usual response and all was well. Out of the darkness a voice appeared on the frequency and said in monotone, "Learjets. Dallas Cowboys. No wonder football tickets cost so much." Then he disappeared into the night.

Lear One Dallas Cowboys had more than the allotted 15 minutes of fame. It was famous every day and every night. So is its owner.

54

CAP'N RICK AND COMPANY

American Airlines did an outstanding job of flying the Dallas Cowboys to their away games. The cream of their pilot crop flew those types of flights. The entire team, coaches, select staff and media were all onboard one American Airlines 727. If that airplane had ever gone down with the entire Dallas Cowboys football team, it would not be due to the well-worn phrase "pilot error." Captain Rick Weiler was "the best." I am proud to call him a friend.

After the Cowboys 34-28 win against the New York Giants on Sunday, September 13, 1992, we departed from Teterboro, New Jersey. The Teterboro Airport was not only a mere nine miles from midtown Manhattan but it was close to Giants Stadium. It was where a majority of corporate aircraft that flew into the New York area landed. The team arrived and departed from nearby Newark International in Newark, New Jersey. The New Jersey Giants seemed more appropriate.

We departed Falcon Jet at Teterboro and were climbing out of 17,000 feet while leaving the immediate New

Jerry Jones and the "New Regime"

York area enroute to Dallas. New York City has a lot of Cowboys fans. One would think with two NFL teams, the Jets and the Giants, they would choose one or the other. It made no difference how many teams New York called home prior to the game that day. Eddy and I were outside the breezeway headed toward the visiting coaches booth. A fan walked up and offered me $100 for the official Cowboys windbreaker I was wearing. He wanted to buy it right off my back! The Dallas Cowboys were very popular in the Big Apple.

Several of the air traffic controllers that afternoon were Giants fans, however. They were well-aware of Jerry's insistence, ego and his push toward the forefront. As we flew toward Dallas after the game we were in trail, which meant we had departed shortly after the American charter that carried the team. Since we were both on the same flight plan route home, the controllers began talking back and forth between us, giving us some good-natured teasing.

It all started when Rick and Company first checked in with Center. "New York Center, good afternoon, this is Cowboys charter, American 913, out of one-seven-thousand and cleared to flight level two-three-zero," he said. I checked in several seconds after they did, "New York Center, Lear One Dallas Cowboys, we're out of one-five-thousand climbing to flight level two-three-zero," I said. They were slightly ahead of us during their climb out but they knew we would soon catch and pass them once we arrived at our filed cruise altitude.

Center responded to Eddy and I whimsically with "You mean you've got the team in front...and the owner behind! Lear One Dallas Cowboys that 727 is pulling away from you guys," he said. "Yeah, it must be that extra engine," Rick spoke up and said. The Boeing 727 they flew was a "three holer" meaning it had three jet engines where the Lear was a two-engine airplane. It would not make any difference at altitude because of the power to weight ratio. Very few airplanes performed like a Learjet.

Everyone laughed at the New York controllers obvious familiarity with the Cowboys flamboyant owner. I spoke up and said, "That's not the reason you guys are beating us. It's because of the steroids!" They were the ones carrying the team. The controller laughed and we continued on to Dallas as the Cowboys flamboyant owner enjoyed another victory.

Slowly but surely, the Dallas Cowboys took a back seat to Jerry Jones. Perhaps now more than ever....

55

COACH 'EM

Most of the actual coaching during the games comes from the coaches booth, via headset, to the sidelines. If the Cowboys won or lost, it sometimes depended upon the strategies from the booth. It was truly the 1990's and professional football was high tech. Robert Blackwell, the Cowboys Video Director and his associates climbed into their respective stadium perches on game day high atop the gridiron action. They filmed each and every play of each and every game, each and every Sunday. Rain or shine.

It was impossible for any one coach to see and make the "adjustments" necessary to win from the sidelines. From Mr. Blackwell's vantage point, everything was seen. Every formation, every potential strength and weakness of their opponents. Before each play the camera "locked in" on the field. Automatically a 6x8 black and white print of every players position was instantly available for the coaches in the box to review. That meant that when the offense was on the field, Dave Wannstedt would review the photos, maybe spot a weakness or tendency and constantly adjust his scheme for the next defensive series of plays. Same for Norv Turner's offense.

In the visiting coaches booth at all the away games sat Dave Wannstedt, Robert Ford, Joe Brodsky and Norv Turner. Bruce Mays seemed to always be there, as did Mike Woicik. When space was available I always tried to sit there, too. I thought "fair weather fans" got excited, mad and upset during a football game. Try the "normal" conversations in the Dallas Cowboys coaches booth. It was interesting and exciting to say the least. I even learned some new four-letter words!

Joe Brodsky was the running backs coach. He was Emmitt Smith's mentor. He was a very colorful character and an exceptional coach. Joe was also a very vocal personality. He called it like he saw it. During the Cowboys merciless 31-7 shellacking by the Philadelphia Eagles at Veterans Stadium on Monday, October 5, 1992, Joe had apparently seen quite enough.

What he saw was Emmitt Smith not hitting the holes. Emmitt normally never had that problem, he would hit them straight in and hard. He has proven that. In this particular game, however, God-given talent and ability alone were not getting the job done.

A few plays later Joe had definitely seen enough. He called down to the sidelines for Tony Wise, the Cowboys offensive line coach. "Tony, you tell number 22 if he doesn't start hitting the holes, I'm gonna take his ass out of there," Joe yelled into the headset. "Joe, you know, you know, that Emmitt doesn't like anyone to tell him what to do during the game," Tony replied.

"I don't give a goddamn, you tell him! You tell him I said if he doesn't start hitting the holes, I'm gonna find somebody who will," Joe bellowed. "Ah Joe, I don't want to make him mad," Wise answered. "You tell him, you tell him now! I don't care who he is," Joe yelled back.

From my vantage point I couldn't really see the Cowboys sideline. I never noticed whether Tony told Emmitt or not. Superstar players were still people and they all had their little quirks. One of Emmitt's was that he doesn't like for anyone to "mess" with him during the game. Emmitt knew how to play the game of football. I'm willing to bet Tony didn't say a word. Tony dealt with the offensive line that supposedly created the holes....

On game day Emmitt is in the "zone." Unfortunately for the Cowboys opponents he is usually in their END zone.

56

HAPPY BIRTHDAY TO ME!

It was October 24, 1992, my 26th birthday and I was actually upset that Eddy and I would not be flying Lear One Dallas Cowboys to Los Angeles for the Cowboys vs. Raiders game. I had become friends with a couple of the L.A. Raiderette cheerleaders two years ago. Since we flew to the west coast quite often, I had stayed more than in touch with Cheryl. I was going to miss the chance for her to give me my birthday "present." For the Raiders game Jerry had arranged an American Airlines 757 instead of the customary 727. The reason? A group of additional media, corporate sponsors, VIPs and select friends were invited to the game.

Eddy and I flew with Jerry from Dallas to Springdale, Arkansas, to pick up Don Tyson. Tyson, as in Tyson/Holly Farms Foods. Don was a friend and fellow back-scratcher of Jerry's. We flew him and his party to Love Field so they could join the rest of the royalty for the flight to Los Angeles. There should have been a limousine waiting at Jet East to take them to the designated area on the west ramp at Dallas/Fort Worth International, where the Cowboys always departed for away games.

I will never, the coaches will never, the staffers will never and I'm sure many of the players will agree, understand Jerry Jones financial philosophies. He was spending a large amount of money for an American Airlines 757. He also arranged to fly his private Learjet to Arkansas and back. On the other hand, Jerry was too cheap to hire a limousine for Mr. Tyson and his group. I never understood that.

Jet East had a limousine but a blue 1985 Cadillac was not exactly all a man could hope for. As everyone deplaned, "Todd, can you drive that limousine, you think you can handle it?" Jerry asked. No, Jerry, I'm sure it's far superior, technologically, to the Learjet but why not, I thought. "Of course I can," I replied. Maybe.

I have enough pilots licenses to wallpaper my bedroom. I did not have a license to drive limousines, but what the hell. I'll try just about anything once. As my birthday present from Jerry Jones I became a stretch limousine driver. We loaded their luggage, everyone climbed in and I fired that baby up.

We were well on our way to Dallas/Fort Worth International Airport when Mr. Tyson asked, "Todd, we've got a couple of hours, is there a restaurant or bar to stop off and pass some time?" They were not in any hurry. "Well, there is a Humperdink's in Las Colinas. Claims to have the 'World's Tallest Bar'. A lot of the Cowboys go there after a game. Plus, its on the way," I replied. "That'll be fine," Don said, and Humperdink's it was.

I have to admit that driving a stretch limousine was not like anything I had ever done before but we made it to Humperdink's and I was set to wait it out in the limo.

Happy Birthday To Me!

"Don't be silly, you don't have any more flying to do today, do you? Come on in with us and I'll buy you a drink for your birthday," Don insisted. Well, maybe it would help ease the pain of not being able to unwrap Cheryl in Los Angeles. "Okay," I replied.

Don found out it was my birthday when I was handling the meetin' and greetin' in Springdale at Springdale Air Services. He made the mistake of asking me how I was doing and I told him, "I'm doing great. Today is my birthday."

We had more than a couple of birthday drinks and some real tasty chicken appetizers. We piled back into that ratty Jet East limousine and pulled up to the right ramp at the right airport.

As I pulled up to the charter everyone scrambled out and checked in their luggage. "Todd, I know you're not a limo driver. Thanks for everything. I hope you enjoy your birthday." Mr. Tyson said. He handed me $200.

For once, I was glad that Jerry Jones steps on a dollar to pick up a dime. Birthdays are special days and that was one I will always remember.

57

PISS ON 'YA!

A person might tend to wonder if they were partners in crime. William Jefferson Clinton and Jerral Wayne Jones. Two good 'ol boys from Arkansas. Jerry did a lot of back-scratching with several wealthy Arkansans, but not that one. My first clue was late one evening at Central Flying Service in Little Rock.

During the course of his presidential campaign, then Governor Clinton had chartered several Express One 727s. They flew across the United States on the campaign trail. His campaign manager flew on one of the airliners and he and his staff flew on another. Many times when we arrived in Little Rock they were parked at Central.

One night we flew a "girlfriend" trip to "the pebble." Jerry and his main-squeeze, Susan, stumbled out of Lear One Dallas Cowboys and she quickly headed toward the terminal and the little girl's room. Other than the painful urge of "nature's call" they were both feeling real good. Across the tarmac, parked in the distance, sat one of Clinton's Express One 727s. Jerry stood there talking to

Jerry Jones and the "New Regime"

Eddy and I as he took a whiz on the ramp, right next to the left wing. In front of God and everybody!

When reporters weren't around Jerry never kept his feelings to himself and that was no different. He began rambling on about Clinton. "I hope that son of a bitch doesn't get it," he drawled. "God, if he's our next president, we're in for a world of trouble," he said. Nowhere near the amount of trouble that Jerry would have been in if Gene had known where he was that night. Jerry knew all about trouble. He was never afraid.

One would think that he and now President Clinton would be friends because they had a lot of things in common. They were both from Arkansas, both liked the comfort and convenience of private airplanes and each liked the spotlight, famous friends and beautiful women. Also, both of their characters and business practices were called in to question on a regular basis.

I guess I should have known they were nothing alike. Jerry liked to keep his money and Clinton always tries to take some of it. Jerry resides in Dallas and President Clinton resides in The White House. The way those two have proven to be, it was easy to see that Arkansas was just not big enough for the two of 'em.

In my countless travels with Jerry, I for the first time, sensed a different tone in his voice. I had heard his often scathing, critical and frustrated comments a thousand times before. That type of backlash was normally reserved for his "make-believe" friend, Jimmy Johnson. After a few beverages, however, the truth always came out. Bourbon and Diet Coke was Jerry Jones truth serum.

It was a tone of jealousy. He was the king of Arkansas. He was The Man. No longer was he the only famous son of Little Rock. He was in complete control of a burgeoning football dynasty. He was one of the wealthiest men in America and had gained the respect of his NFL peers. Jerry Jones was not above petty jealousy.

What could be next from the great state of Arkansas...The Anti-Christ?

58

FIRST TIME FOR EVERYTHING

If ever in the position of entertaining Jerry Jones, make sure there is plenty of bourbon and Diet Coke. It also wouldn't hurt to be royalty, a famous movie star or just plain beautiful. Like Mr. Bojangles says in the song, he "drinks a bit."

The only time I ever saw him turn down a drink was in Stuttgart, Arkansas. After the Cowboys convincing 30-3 win over the New York Giants on Thanksgiving day in 1992, Eddy and I flew the family to Little Rock and dropped off the better halves. Jerry, Stephen, Shy and McCoy—all the men in the family, so to speak—continued on to the "Duck Club" for a big after-Thanksgiving holiday hunt.

They always enjoyed a Cowboys victory. In other words, before we departed late that evening, they all had more than a couple of pre-departure beverages. Of course, on the flight there, they were having a good time, too.

Jerry always mixed a bourbon and Diet Coke for the road. After we landed in Stuttgart, as they loaded their guns into the van for the drive to the club, Eddy asked Jerry about a "supposed to" departure time for the following day. Like it ever made any difference. The boss was never late; the flight crew was always early.

"Jerry, do you need anything?" I asked him as they prepared to leave. "Yeah, Todd, why don't you fix me a drink for the road, bourbon and Diet Coke," he drawled. I fixed him a fresh one inside Lear One Dallas Cowboys and handed it to him. "No, maybe I better not," he said. I couldn't believe it.

"Well, now I know that there really is a first time for everything. Jerry Jones just turned down a drink," I joked. Jerry smiled his infectious smile and everyone just burst out laughing. Score one for the co-pilot. They climbed in the van and went on their merry way. Jerry had a great sense of humor and he knew that was a good one.

Isn't it always the little things that seem to grow into the huge monsters? As I think back on Jerry's world, the list of items that could have changed the course of Dallas Cowboys history was mind-numbing. During my tenure I flew him to NFL owners meetings all over the country. I'm thankful I wasn't there on that fateful night in Orlando in March of 1994.

It was inevitable...we knew that. But what if Jerry had expressed the same sentiments on that night as he had at the "Duck Club?" Sadly, we will never know. I'm willing to bet that Jerry, Jimmy, the hardest working coaching staff in the NFL and the Dallas Cowboys may have shared in their own piece of football history—a Super Bowl "three-peat."

If only Jerry Jones "first time for everything" had been in Orlando.

59

CALIFORNIA DREAMIN'

An unfortunate event occurred on January 9, 1993, during the Cowboys bye week and prior to their N.F.C. Championship game against the San Francisco 49ers at Candlestick Park. I was involved in a traffic accident and broke my nose. It was semi-serious and required almost four hours of reconstructive surgery. After the Cowboys victory over the team of the 80's, it represented a changing of the guard. I, however, felt like an injured player that had battled for his chance to finally attend a Super Bowl and was told he couldn't play. It never stopped them and I was determined not to let it stop me, either. I had worked too hard during the past several years for the opportunity to pass me by.

I had flown all over the country at all hours of the day and night. Jerry Jones, Jimmy Johnson, Emmitt Smith, Troy Aikman, Mark Tuinei and James Washington, to name a few, had been entrusted in the flight crew's capable hands. I had unselfishly devoted all of my time and contributed to the cause. I wouldn't miss it. In the past, we had been tremendously busy flying into and out of the Super Bowl. I was thrilled that the Cowboys had achieved the unthinkable. I assumed, however, our flight schedule would be even more mind-boggling than usual. The Super Bowl was in Pasadena, California, and I knew that the flights would be long, difficult and frequent. I didn't care. Against doctors orders I attended Super Bowl XXVII. I deserved to go. I had earned it.

To my and Eddy's pleasant surprise, Jerry made it easy on us. Everyone who had worked so long and hard the past several years in getting the Cowboys to the pinnacle, were able to enjoy a small victory of their own. So often the Dallas Cowboys seemed to be a thankless organization, Jerry proved everyone wrong that time. He chartered an American Airlines 757 for the team. For the cheerleaders, news media, invited guests and employees, an additional DC-10. He even arranged an Express One 727 charter to fly his many long-time oil and gas associates and close friends from Little Rock and Ft. Smith, Arkansas, to Los Angeles for the game.

We departed Dallas/Fort Worth International on January 28, 1993, and flew to Los Angeles International Airport. The team had flown out the week prior to begin the pre-Super Bowl hype. All of the remaining staff, invited guests and cheerleaders were onboard. It was definitely a full airplane. I wasn't looking my best, but I felt good. It was an exciting time for everyone. Upon our arrival in Los Angeles, I learned that the Cowboys had three hotels they were operating out of during the week. The Guest Quarters Suite Hotel for the working staff, The Loews Santa Monica Beach Hotel for the players and coaches, and the Westin Bonaventure for the friends and employees.

California Dreamin'

Transportation was provided via buses to and from the airport as well as the game. Additional transportation times were posted in the main lobby of each hotel for the numerous parties and other special events. In addition to the Cowboys parties, Garth Brooks, Liza Minelli and Richard Pryor performed over the weekend. It was the first of many Super Bowls under the "New Regime" and they did it right. Jerry was in Hollywood and he could not have written a better script. The things that I had seen and experienced, the hatred and the adversity, all seemed like distant and forgotten memories. Jerry Jones was happy. To him, getting there had been half the fun.

The flight to Los Angeles International that morning proved that theory, also. Jerry's "friend" and I had become friends so she arranged to sit next to me on the flight. The son of the legend, Bob Lilly, Jr., was also seated in my row, we had a great time. Among the others were Jerry, Jr. and the Dallas Cowboys cheerleaders. Less than 20 minutes outside of Los Angeles, however, strange and overpowering odors began to emanate from the rear of the Luxuryliner. The odor was so strong that I wondered when the overhead oxygen masks would start dropping. As the passengers began to get curious, we turned around to see the cheerleaders playing "beauty shop" in the rear of the airplane.

Forty-eight different perfumes were mixed with 48 different kinds of hairspray. The girls always looked beautiful but they were definitely from Texas. To borrow a phrase from my friends at American Airlines they were "based here, best hair!" Everyone was reaching for their overhead air controls and laughing. Susan and I were sitting at least 15 rows in front of them but others were

Jerry Jones and the "New Regime"

not as fortunate. I was the lucky one. I couldn't smell anything anyway!

After we landed, everyone deciphered their color-coded luggage tags at baggage claim. I learned I was staying at the Westin Bonaventure in downtown Los Angeles. Everyone who was an employee or invited guest received a welcome packet that contained all of their invitations and tickets. There were events and parties planned for both before and after the game. Everyone was hoping that the after-Super Bowl bash would be the one to remember. So far, the Super Bowl rivaled any event I had ever seen, especially when the Dallas Cowboys were playing.

I wanted to check out the sights and prepare myself for the welcome party that night at the Auditorium. I called several of my friends in California and then I placed a call to my friend, Chad Johnson. He was staying at the team's headquarters in Santa Monica at the Loews Santa Monica Beach Hotel. We made plans to enjoy ourselves during the weekend. Virtually everyone in the Cowboys organization was present at the welcome party that night. Jerry was in rare form. Electricity was in the air. The party ended around 10:00 p.m. and everyone retired early.

We all needed rest because the big bash was just a few days away. I could hardly wait.

60

PASADENA 1993

With so many parties, events and festivities planned around the Super Bowl weekend, it was a busy time for everyone. The mood among the faithful could best be described as casually tense. The players were on a mission. They seemed surprisingly relaxed and confident. Jimmy Johnson was cautiously optimistic and evenly keeled, but he was always like that. Jerry Jones, however, was fit to be tied. He was beside himself with anticipation and excitement. This was his chance, once and for all, to tell America "I told you so." He had known it all along.

There were so many things to do and see that I didn't know where to begin. On Friday I went to Santa Monica and met some fellow employees and joined in on the festivities at the team's hotel. Then we went to Main Street ate a late lunch and checked out the trendy, sophisticated and funky shops in downtown Santa Monica. It was a great day and I couldn't believe I actually had time to stop and enjoy the weekend. Especially a Super

Bowl weekend. I headed back to the hotel early that evening because a special guest was coming by to visit. She wanted to give me a belated birthday present. It was worth the wait.

Cheryl and I ate a late lunch and went to the Super Bowl parade in downtown Los Angeles on Saturday afternoon. I had made plans to hit the town with Chad Johnson. Around 9:00 p.m. I headed toward Santa Monica. As I walked through the lobby, the party had already started in the bar of the Loews Santa Monica Beach Hotel. I spotted a friend of mine, Ron Thornton, who worked in ticket sales at the stadium. We had a quick beer and I went upstairs to the suite. I had never seen a suite that big. It was HUGE! Jimmy had exclusive use of a complimentary limo which he allowed Chad and I to use for the evening.

Unfortunately, after a few phone calls we were unable to get in touch with Rhonda. She had confiscated the limo for some shopping and dinner, and we did not know when she was coming back. Chad called a friend from Dallas who had transferred to L.A. recently and she came to pick us up. We headed to a well-known and prominent club in L.A., then drove to Manhattan Beach.

It was a zoo everywhere we went. I had proof. It was virtually impossible to get to the bar. Chad and I were standing there when a conversation began with a fella standing next to us. He rambled on about the Cowboys and then made a remark about Jimmy's hair. He looked at Chad, "You know what? His hair looks a lot like yours does," he said. He had no idea that Chad was Jimmy's son! Chad didn't think it was very funny but I thought it was hilarious; so did she.

The buses headed to Pasadena at noon on Sunday, January 31. When we arrived and I located my seats in the 105,000 seat Rose Bowl, I couldn't believe it. I had one of the best seats in the house! The sun was shining brightly and it was perfect football weather. I walked down on the sidelines and talked with several Cowboys prior to the game. Electricity was in the air as I looked around the monstrous stadium. I had a seat on the 45 yard line, Cowboys side, 23 rows up. It was showtime! The Dallas Cowboys vs. the Buffalo Bills. Super Bowl XXVII.

As kickoff time approached, I was amazed at the number of Cowboys fans in the stadium. The actress Dyan Cannon and her beautiful daughter sat two rows in front of me. I saw the recently unemployed Mike Ditka and I met Patti Labelle while waiting in line for a 16 oz. $5 beer. It was an experience of a lifetime and I was there. The "New Regime" had overcome all odds. It seemed like only yesterday when we were 1-15. As Garth Brooks sang the national anthem and as the jets flew overhead the crowd erupted in cheers.

As I sat down, I noticed that one of the major sponsors of the game, GTE, had provided a souvenir seat cushion for everyone to sit on—105,000 of them! In addition to the graphics on the outside, I unzipped the pocket and it was full of goodies on the inside. Game Day collector's cards and a mini stereo with headphones for listening to the game. Oh, and of course, my 2'x 2' folded cardboard sheet for the halftime show. Michael Jackson's elaborate spectacle would make an attempt to "Heal the World." We played our part by holding up colored cards at the designated time to form children for the worldwide television audience. It was a creative idea.

It was a blowout as the Cowboys rumbled to a 52-17 victory. The fans were talking about that show-off Leon Lett. Troy Aikman was named MVP while Jim Kelly pouted after his injury. The Dallas Cowboys were the world champions. Jerry Jones was on the sidelines almost to the point of tears. They had done it! He and Jimmy had rebuilt the once proud Dallas Cowboys and emerged from the ashes. I helped him accomplish that feat without ever even realizing what we had done. I felt pride and a great sense of personal satisfaction. Even though Eddy and I were exhausted as a flight crew, I felt it was all worthwhile. I will never forget being a part of it.

I thought the Dallas Cowboys put on a show during the game. The after-Super Bowl bash was unbelievable. It was held at the Santa Monica Civic Auditorium. After the game everyone was shuttled back to their hotels. I changed, showered and dressed to impress. It was open bar and party time! Gary Busey, Gene Hackman and Tanya Tucker were there. Tanya sang "Take the Ribbon From Your Hair" to Jerry. I talked with Dave Wannstedt and congratulated him on his new job as Head Coach of the Bears. I mingled and sat in the VIP area with Jimmy and Chad.

The emotion was tremendous in the room as Jerry and Jimmy gave their speeches. I finally left at 4:00 a.m. (shortly before everyone was naked and dancing on the tables) I knew that the buses departed for the airport promptly at 9:00 a.m. It all seemed like a dream. I can only imagine how Jimmy must have felt. I knew all too well how Jerry felt.

Many of the players didn't stay very long at the postgame party. They had their own private parties planned, no doubt. Jerry Jones finally went to the Super Bowl and took the team with him. Upon our arrival at the Los Angeles International Airport the following morning, there was many a hangover and tired partygoer as our police escort shuttled us through to the private area for departure. The hangovers prevailed. Everyone slept.

When a pilot retires or achieves something special, it was customary to do one thing. They sprayed arcs of water over the airplane as we arrived. It was a nice gesture for everyone who had worked so hard to make the Cowboys successful. I only wish I could have been a part of it the following year, too. But Jerry was finally able to arrive with the team, the boos were less frequent and the spotlight loomed larger than ever. He had heard his wakeup call. The first of many Super Bowls was under his belt, as well as Jimmy's. The much criticized and scrutinized owner had persevered. The Dallas Cowboys were World Champions!

Jerry was vindicated. Jimmy had conquered. I felt like a world champion, too.

EPILOGUE

    I proudly sat in the Rose Bowl on January 31, 1993, as the Cowboys returned to, and successfully won, their first Super Bowl title since 1977. Following the 1993 season, and after Super Bowl XXVIII, they owned back-to-back world championships. No organization worked harder for success. I know. Jimmy Johnson put it best when he said, "The harder we work, the luckier we get."

    Many prominent names and famous faces have entered Jerry Jones revolving door at Valley Ranch and never looked back. Former Head Coach Jimmy Johnson's inevitable, and not surprising departure, was sealed during a tumultuous off-season. Dave Wannstedt and his close friend, Tony Wise, now guide the Chicago Bears. Norv Turner is rebuilding the Washington Redskins and Butch Davis now leads the University of Miami.

    Life, big-business, and most certainly professional football, remained a volatile and ever-changing world, as I soon found out. Shortly after the "New Regime's" first Super Bowl victory, I was also placed on waivers. I was called in and abruptly laid off due to a drastic reduction in Jerry's flight schedule. There was no warning. The bean-counters had won. He decided to fly with the team on the American Airlines charters for next season.

Eddy managed to salvage his job at the last minute. I, on the other hand, was expendable. In an effort to ease my shock, Eddy quickly pointed out that I had done nothing wrong—I stayed loyal, I stuck it out through thick and thin, I respected my peers, I sacrificed, I did my job under the most adverse conditions, and I did it with a smile. Didn't matter. What Eddy didn't know was that the words, "We are going to have to let you go," evoked a strange mixture of feelings. I was both surprised and at the same time, I felt relieved.

My intimate experiences with Jerry Jones and the Dallas Cowboys suddenly came to a close. Jerry and the entire Cowboys organization did provide a lifetime of memoirs and recollections, however. This book represents a small fraction of those. I must say, through all the adversity, heartache, good times, bad times and ugly times, I am thrilled to have played even a small part.

My favorite team unfolded right in front of my eyes. Every player, every game, scouting trip, business and pleasure flight, contributed to their ultimate success. I enjoyed my years with the Dallas Cowboys and I can honestly say that it was all I ever imagined it would be...and then some. I will never view professional sports in the same way ever again.

I witnessed first-hand more than an inside view of "America's Team." I gained knowledge, friendships and experience that I will benefit from for the rest of my life. The reality of things, however, is they change everyday. One must be prepared. Life with Jerry Jones and the

Epilogue

Dallas Cowboys helped me to do that. I grew as a person and learned that the ability to adapt is what keeps one alive.

Left alone with my thoughts and observations, I came to several conclusions about Jerry Jones as an individual. As I climbed into bed in some strange hotel room, I often reflected on the events of the day and I quietly analyzed them in my mind. I was sometimes amazed at the personality, psyche and eccentricities of Jerral Wayne Jones. The ancient proverb, "Actions speak louder than words" consistently held true.

Jerry Jones always has, and always will, push it to the limit. The National Football League, commissioner Paul Tagliabue, other NFL owners, coaches, players, staffers, fans, and Jerry's family would be well-served to take notes.

Jerry Jones portrayed a profound sense of dissatisfaction with his own accomplishments. He used success, victory, conflict and confrontation as a catalyst to greater ambition. Each and every goal that he accomplished became a stepping-stone toward a more "unattainable" one. Just like the Cowboys "Get up" for a big game, under adversity Jerry did the same thing. He consistently performed at his highest level—when the stakes were highest.

Jerry also possessed a killer instinct. He secretly delighted in conflict. He often appeared to distort reality to serve some sort of competitive purpose. Business is a competition, and an almost exclusive head game. Jerry always seemed to enjoy coming from behind, even if the score indicated he was destroying his opponent.

The Dallas Cowboys will always hold a special place in my heart. They are not just "America's Team" anymore—they are "My Team" and one that I am proud to have been associated with. The most valuable lesson I learned from Jerry, however, was his own business philosophy. It is the same philosophy that he uses daily to persevere, endure and finish what he starts. My days and nights behind the controls of Lear One Dallas Cowboys were not for naught because I know now—Business Really Is Business. I was afforded a rare opportunity to witness the master up close and in person. Perhaps, Jerry Jones taught me too well....

"Think with your head and not with your heart."

Send $22.95 plus $3.95 shipping/handling charge for each book ordered to:
TTHORN Publishing, Inc.
P.O. Box 630232
Irving, Texas 75063

To order by phone, call 1-800-711-2338

☐ Yes, I wish to order _____ copies of *Jerry Jones and the "New Regime"*

Name_____

Address_____

City_____ State_____ Zip_____

☐ Enclosed find check or money order in the amount of $_____ made payable to TTHORN PUBLISHING, INC.

☐ I wish to charge my order on my ☐ Visa ☐ Mastercard

Acct. No._____ Exp. Date_____

(Signature) _____

Send $22.95 plus $3.95 shipping/handling charge for each book ordered to:
TTHORN Publishing, Inc.
P.O. Box 630232
Irving, Texas 75063

To order by phone, call 1-800-711-2338

☐ Yes, I wish to order _____ copies of *Jerry Jones and the "New Regime"*

Name_____

Address_____

City_____ State_____ Zip_____

☐ Enclosed find check or money order in the amount of $_____ made payable to TTHORN PUBLISHING, INC.

☐ I wish to charge my order on my ☐ Visa ☐ Mastercard

Acct. No._____ Exp. Date_____

(Signature) _____

Send $22.95 plus $3.95 shipping/handling charge for each book ordered to:

TTHORN Publishing, Inc.
P.O. Box 630232
Irving, Texas 75063

To order by phone, call 1-800-711-2338

☐ Yes, I wish to order _____ copies of *Jerry Jones and the "New Regime"*

Name_____

Address_____

City_____ State_____ Zip_____

☐ Enclosed find check or money order in the amount of $_____ made payable to TTHORN PUBLISHING, INC.

☐ I wish to charge my order on my ☐ Visa ☐ Mastercard

Acct. No._____Exp. Date_____

(Signature) _____

Send $22.95 plus $3.95 shipping/handling charge for each book ordered to:

TTHORN Publishing, Inc.
P.O. Box 630232
Irving, Texas 75063

To order by phone, call 1-800-711-2338

☐ Yes, I wish to order _____ copies of *Jerry Jones and the "New Regime"*

Name_____

Address_____

City_____ State_____ Zip_____

☐ Enclosed find check or money order in the amount of $_____ made payable to TTHORN PUBLISHING, INC.

☐ I wish to charge my order on my ☐ Visa ☐ Mastercard

Acct. No._____Exp. Date_____

(Signature) _____